MEETING YOUR MATCH

A Practical Guide
For
Finding Your Perfect Mate

By
Karen A. Bowen

Published in the United States of America by
Ariadne Publishers, Brookfield, WI, U.S.A. © 1995
and 2019. All rights reserved.

ISBN: 9780964934306

TABLE OF CONTENTS
Part One

Part Two

A True Story

Dedication

To the Christ, the guiding light of my life.

Acknowledgments

I acknowledge with love and a grateful heart: Yogacharya Oliver Black without whose example, unconditional love, and relentless guidance I would not have awakened in this life. Richard A. Bowen without whose presence and love I could not have achieved the goal. Sharon McCarragher whose insight and suggestions made this book possible. And to all the friends and teachers along the way who inspired me to keep on keeping on.

"You will teach others to find their perfect partners, for there is so much pain and suffering caused by mismatched couples."

Preface

This book is a wake-up call, reminding you of the underlying principles you must honor to fulfill your dreams. Although the book is directed at those seeking their perfect partner, the seven keys can be used to achieve any worthwhile goal, for they are based upon Universal laws. When we cooperate with these laws, life is beautiful and full of joy. When we break the laws, life breaks us.

We all have a history; I call it our legacy. The life we fashion from it depends on whether we use our past experiences as stepping stones or as stumbling blocks. The good news is that each of us can awaken right now, and change our lives totally and completely. We can live our dreams and become that great and noble being we were put here to be. It is all up to us. Each of us.

Ultimately, the goal of this book is to help you find much more than the *Love of a Lifetime*. By becoming proficient in these simple ideas, you will truly become the master of your own destiny.

Karen A. Bowen

♥ ♥ ♥ ♥ ♥ ♥ ♥ ♥ ♥ ♥ ♥ ♥

We wish you Godspeed in finding the relationship that makes your heart sing — the match that exceeds all expectations and desires. Our hearts are with you. Never, ever quit.

Karen and Richard Bowen

Part One

Seven Keys

for

Finding Your Perfect Mate

Finding True Love

is not a matter

of trial and error.

It is the result

of being true

to oneself.

Chapter One

THE GOAL

The primary objective of this book is to prepare you to meet your ideal partner, nothing less. With that in mind, the first question then becomes:

WHAT IS A PERFECT PARTNER?

A perfect partner is tailor-made for you, just like the right- and left-hand gloves in a pair. It is a relationship of equals and lovers, of playmates and confidantes. Perfect partners are certain they belong together, that there is not a better match waiting "out there, somewhere" if this one doesn't work.

Perfect partners harmonize mentally, physically and spiritually. Both partners believe that the other is the greatest person they could have ever chosen. Their relationship is delightful, and gets better with time and experience. They offer one another solace in the storms of life. In fact, one of the best signs of perfect pairing is that they are always sweethearts.

In the perfect pair, no changes are required. In other words, they like each other just the way they are, and don't feel a need to "work at" the relationship or change one another. This does not preclude growth or improvement, but desire for growth comes to each partner from within, instead of from outside themselves.

Since the individuals feel safe, nourished, at-home, and natural with one another, there is no need for pretense. Even during disagreements, both partners know their relationship is secure, because it is based upon a mutual desire for respect, caring, and kindness. Both want open and honest communication, even if emotionally painful.

Perfect partners are synergistic. They come to each other whole, but can accomplish much more together by complementing one another. No compromises that lead to mediocrity are required. Instead, both individuals regard their partner's needs equally, and decisions are based upon what is highest and best for both.

Perfect partners treat each other like the best of friends and truly look forward to being together. When they are in each other's arms, it is like no other relationship has ever been ...a meeting of the mind, heart and soul as well as body.

The process of finding your perfect partner is often opposite that of normal relationships, in which you find someone to whom you are attracted, get to know the person, and then make a commitment. Often, normal relationships are characterized by a meteoric climb to climax, only to fall back to earth with a thud. In contrast, when you recognize your perfect partner, it is natural to make the commitment first (Richard and I were married within 3 months), then get to know one another. The relationship between perfect partners expands and gets better with time, offering more fulfillment with each experience.

In the examples of perfect pairing we have seen, one basic trait is constant in each couple: they know they are perfect for one another. One couple met in high school and were married when they were eighteen years old. When I asked how they knew they were right for one another, the wife replied, "My mother made one point clear about choosing a mate. She said, 'Never choose one that you don't like just the way he is.' When I met Mel, I just thought he was great, and he felt the same way about me." This couple has been married for over forty years. Through the ups and downs of having five children and running a family business, they have remained sweethearts. The last time I saw them, at a weekend retreat, they were cuddling as they sat on the floor near the fireplace and listened to a lecture.

WHY ARE YOU HERE?

"What do you want in a relationship?" That's the first question I ask any new client. It seems simple, but the answer most often resembles a list of options on the window sticker of a new vehicle: she has to be cute, he has to be Jewish, someone with similar interests, she has to be athletic and have nice legs, he has to have a college education, non-smoker, she can't have kids, there has to be this "chemistry," has to have money, must have a good job, a pretty smile, dances cool, good in bed, and on and on.

The next question I ask: "Have you ever dated someone with the attributes that are on your checklist?" The answer is almost unanimous, "Yes, but it didn't work out, because..." I then listen to a litany of reasons why the partner fit the checklist, but had other defects. Frequently, the client has had several similar relationships, all with people who fit the checklist, but who didn't work out.

So, where is the problem?

Love is of the heart, not the mind.

These individuals treat love, romance and marriage like the purchase of a car or an entertainment center, and then wonder why the relationship ends in disaster. Instead of seeking a lifetime partner, they seem to be shopping for a companion who will keep them amused and entertained, perhaps so they won't have to experience the emptiness that lies within themselves.

Turning the tables, I then ask these same individuals how they would feel if a partner chose them only for their looks, their financial condition, or any of the other items on their own checklist. Again, the answer is almost unanimous: "No, I want someone to love me for who I am, not for what I look like or for what I own." Amazingly, this is often the first time in our interview that the word "love" is mentioned.

CAN I HELP YOU?

It is at this point in our first session that I explain to a new client:

"You can have any kind of relationship you desire, but you don't need me to help you find another mediocre, unhappy, or abusive match. I can only be of assistance if you want to meet your perfect match. By perfect, I mean the partner who harmonizes with you in every way — mentally, physically and spiritually. The partner who is tailor-made for you.

"If you want the partner who loves you just the way you are, who thinks you are the most wonderful person in the world...if you want a relationship that exceeds your wildest and sweetest dreams...if you want a relationship that grows sweeter and more loving with time and experience, then we can work together. Success is guaranteed, if you want what is highest and best for you in your life."

Where do we begin?

The first rule of success is to be in the right place at the right time. But how do you accomplish that?

In music, voices or instruments which harmonize do not play the same notes. They play certain notes which complement each other. As these differing musical notes weave together, rather than creating mere noise or discordance, they blend to become a beautiful ballad, energetic jazz, or a stimulating rhapsody.

The same rapport can be achieved in relationships, but to find the one who harmonizes with you, you must be playing your own tune. You have to be your true self — the natural you, with no pretense, no polite veneer of feigned interest, no disguises.

To this end, you must begin the journey toward meeting your perfect partner by discarding your old, limiting thoughts and beliefs about yourself, what you can have, and what you deserve in life. The seven keys you will find in this book can help you unlock the doors to the uniqueness of your own being. When you are genuine, your actions are sincere, and you naturally attract the partner who was made just for you.

Summary

PERFECT PARTNERS

1. *Both* partners *know* they belong together.
2. The relationship is synergistic.
3. Both partners think the other is the greatest person they could have ever chosen, just the way he or she is.
4. Their relationship is delightful to both parties and gets better with time and experiences.
5. Both feel very safe, nourished, at-home, and natural.
6. They can be themselves; no pretense is necessary.
7. Each is respectful of the other.
8. The relationship is safe all the time, even in disagreements.
9. Each individual is totally satisfied with the other; there is no desire to look around anymore.
10. No compromises are required.
11. No "working on the relationship" is required.
12. They treat each other like sweethearts.
13. When they are in each other's arms, it is like no other relationship has ever been.
14. They really look forward to being with one another.
15. Both desire open and honest communication.

So, the goal is to be in the right place at the right time to meet your perfect match. And now you have a better idea of what to expect in your relationship. The next question is: "How will you know when you meet the right one?"

Why fritter away your life with mediocrity when highest and best is easier to find?

There are only two ways
to experience life.
You either live to the highest and best,
or settle for something less.

Out of the millions of options, only
one path leads to a life of beauty,
love, and accomplishment.

That path is found by following your
heart; by being true to yourself
in every aspect of life.

Chapter Two

DESIRE

All the Universe operates by law. There is no chaos, only harmony. Being a part of the Uni-verse or "One song," we are subject to its laws. When we cooperate with these laws, we enjoy happiness and prosperity. If we break the laws, we suffer misery and poverty of purse, mind, and experience.

Desire is the motivating force behind every action. From the moment we arise in the morning, each thing we do is goaded and guided by desire. You open your eyes because you have a desire to wake up or perhaps to look at the clock. You set the alarm because of the desire to be on time for work or an appointment. Each piece of clothing you wear fulfills your desire to appear attractive, successful, sexy, thin, athletic, or fashionable. The type of communication you choose satisfies your desire to maintain friendly or hostile relations. The effort you put forth in your work represents your desire for success or failure. Every achievement in life begins with desire. In fact, we get exactly what we "go for" in life. And the quality of our accomplishments are a direct result of the caliber of our original desire. "Ask and ye shall receive. Seek and ye shall find. Knock and it shall be opened unto you." But what are you asking for? What are you seeking? Where are you knocking? What is the quality of your desire?

One man who attended our workshop was a sculptor who created beautiful statues and fountains for lobbies, atriums, and landscaped outdoor gardens. When I asked him if he wanted his perfect partner, he replied, "I don't know." I knew this gentleman would never settle for less than perfection in his work, and I wondered why he was so ambivalent about the kind of relationship he wanted. To be a successful sculptor, he must have a clear mental image of exactly how he wants his work to take form, even before he touches the first piece of material. But here he was, telling me he wasn't sure what kind of relationship he wanted. The problem with that attitude is: the Universe can only give you what you ask for.

"There are only two ways to experience life.
You either live to the highest and best
or settle for something less."

Therefore, the first key is: **you must have a desire for your perfect partner**. But desires come in all sizes and kinds. There is the desire for a pizza, a new car, success, fame, relief from pain, or just a little solitude on a Saturday afternoon. What kind of desire, then, is required for you to find the perfect partner?

Desire can be defined as *a longing for something that promises enjoyment or satisfaction.* But to find your perfect partner, you must have a *heart's desire...* a desire rising from the bottom of your heart, that will not let you go.

An expanded version of the **first key** then becomes: *You Must Have a Heart's Desire for the Perfect Mate,* and nothing less, regardless of their physical, financial, or social situation.

I remember the first time I heard this idea. After my two sad "mis-marriages," my minister cautioned me not to make physical attraction so important, saying, "You have to get past outer appearance. When you meet the right man, you will not be attracted to him because of his looks. Instead, something else will bring you together and then, later, you will notice that he is also attractive."

Somehow, from his statement, I got the idea that the Universe was about to play a trick on me, that my perfect partner would turn out to be someone whose looks I found repulsive. At the time, I did not realize that, because I had certain criteria for the men I dated, there were many individuals I was actually not even open to considering as a partner. In other words, I was limiting myself.

So the **desire** must be for the right person, nothing else. Now, how do you make sure that your desire is just that? Well, here comes the first big difference in action you need to take toward accomplishing your goal:

YOU MUST GIVE UP YOUR CHECKLIST

Yes, you must give up all those beliefs that he or she must be a certain type, with a certain hair color or body shape, with a certain religion or class thereof, and a certain income, or number of children. I know this is in complete contradiction with normal goal-setting plans, which tell you to list all the attributes you want in a partner. But the truth is, you don't have the foggiest idea what your partner is going to be like, so how can you make a list? In fact, your list has probably gotten you into plenty of painful relationships in the past, and that is why you have not yet found the right one. When you decide you are truly tired of all those unfulfilling relationships, the ones that leave you drained and wondering whether love is even worth pursuing, and you finally come to the point where you mean business about finding the *right* one for you, then you have to go about it differently.

When I was searching for my perfect partner, I was caught up in the idea that the right man for me had to look different than I do... so he had to be tall, with dark hair and eyes, macho-masculine build, and probably be older. It never entered my mind at the time that I had already married two men who fit this description. The first time I met Richard, I totally dismissed him as a potential partner because of his strawberry-blonde hair, his slight build, and the fact that he looked 25 years old. I called him "the monk," because he looked as if he never did anything interesting. It took me three years to process through my checklist and give it up before we met again. I had to personally experience the old adage, "Don't judge a book by its cover." It took quite a few first dates and one long "trying to make it happen" relationship before I realized how limiting my checklist was.

GIVING UP YOUR CHECKLIST

Frequently, we do not even know we have a checklist. To help uncover negative beliefs that keep you from finding your perfect mate, make a list of all the things you would like or dislike in a mate. Please note that virtues of kindness, sweetness, gentleness, etc., should not be included.

Now read over each item and become consciously aware of your checklist. Then, use one of the following techniques to release it.

One method of giving up your checklist is to ceremoniously burn it. Another is to look at each item and make a solemn vow that you will not allow that aspect to keep you from your perfect mate. Or, as you review each item, you can bless it and release it. Whatever you do, find a technique that works for you.

It Is Absolutely Imperative
That You Give up
Each Item of Your Checklist
For All Time.
You Can Do this with Your Mind,
As I Have Suggested,
Or the Universe Will Require
That You Do it Through Experience —
The Long, Arduous Path.

In fact, not only do you have to give up your checklist, you must also be willing to accept the right person into your life regardless of their physical, educational, emotional, psychological, or religious traits. In other words, YOU MUST BECOME OPEN AND RECEPTIVE.

Everyone I have spoken with, who has found their perfect mate, agrees that when they met the right one, they found that he or she was more perfect than they could have ever imagined. Richard has qualities that only my heart knew would please me — not my mind. In fact, I could not even have imagined all the wonderful things that he is and does. I didn't know how intricately our lives would entwine until we were married. The truth is, if I had not given up my checklist, I would have missed the opportunity of sharing my life with him.

So, why do you have to give up your checklist? First of all, for the same reason I never suggest that anyone outline a goal— it limits you. Secondly, outer physical characteristics have nothing to do with love. If successful, happy, long-lasting relationships had anything to do with good looks, sexy bodies, or money — then the movie stars in Hollywood would all have great marriages. Third, and most importantly, by giving up your checklist you pave the way to have a love beyond your wildest and sweetest dreams and imaginings.

Often, individuals ask me if they must also quit using creative visualization when they give up their checklist. There are times when creative visualization is appropriate, working in harmony with your growth. I would like to clarify this with an example. When I was overcoming my negative belief that I always had to have a weight problem, I visualized myself as a perfect size 8. This worked in harmony with my highest and best because I knew intuitively that my perfect size, without excess weight, was a size 8. Therefore, I was not limiting myself.

HOWEVER, YOU DO NOT KNOW WHO YOUR PERFECT MATE IS. ALL YOU KNOW IS WHAT YOUR EGO TELLS YOU — YOUR CHECKLIST.

First Key

You Must Have a Heart's Desire
for the Perfect Mate

* Give up all the items on your checklist.

* Become open and receptive.

* Expect your perfect partner to be more than

you could ever dream possible

Affirmation

*I am open and receptive to the one
created just for me.
I take a sacred vow to remove all limits that
have kept us apart.*

"Whatever happens to you,
good or bad,
is your own fault.
Don't blame it on anyone else,
not even God."

Yogacharya Oliver Black

Chapter Three

BELIEF

Over the years, I have met many individuals who say they have the desire for their perfect partner, but simultaneously harbor a belief that they *don't deserve or will never find* the right one. This silent, but deadly, doubt keeps them forever away from the goal. For, the truth is, the Universe can only give you those desires which you believe are possible to attain. Therefore, the SECOND KEY is: *You Must Believe it Is Possible for You to Find Your Perfect Partner.*

The question, then, becomes: how do we change limiting beliefs? I once thought that to change a belief, you had to first know what a belief is, how it is formed, and how it impacts your life. But beliefs are a lot like electricity. We use electricity every day without having a full understanding of what it is, where it comes from, and how it is created. All we have to know is where the switch is. Likewise, all you have to know to change a belief is the basics: what beliefs do, where the pertinent switches are, and how they operate.

THOUGHT AND BELIEF BASICS

Everything that occurs in our lives begins with a *thought*. Before a word can be spoken, it must first exist as a thought. Every act is premeditated, even if the initiating thought only lasts a fleeting nanosecond. But thoughts only become *beliefs* when given energy. *Attention* and *feeling* are the energies

17

we add. A belief, then, is *an idea we have become convinced of.*

Thought + Feeling or Attention = Belief

I once believed that I was a victim of my education, ancestry, religion and experience. Often I would say, "German Shepherds learn to be German Shepherds from German Shepherds." That is a true statement when applied to the canine species or any other animal, for a dog cannot choose to be a cat. Mature humans, however, have the power of thought and the power of will. By those two great powers, we create our destiny. We can thus be anything we make up our minds to be.

Because beliefs are a combination of thoughts and feelings, we have the power to change them. In fact, this change in consciousness is easy. It occurs within us daily, and sometimes moment by moment. Every new piece of information you receive presents an opportunity for you to expand your awareness and to relate differently. Take the realization that perfect partners exist, for example. Before that information was available to me, I thought I had to accept mediocre relationships. As a result, I slogged through one relationship after another, wondering why life had to be so sad. Once the new idea was presented, and I accepted it as a possibility, my whole life changed. Now I recognize that I can have perfection in every area of my life, and I choose not to accept anything less.

This power to change consciousness exists for all of us. You have the power to open up a whole new world, when you choose to change your beliefs. Why? Because these ideas work like mathematics; they are universal principles which anyone can use.

The next part of basic training is the powerful realization that by acting on our beliefs we create our life circumstances. Therefore: change the belief, and you automatically change your life. For example: if, in the past, you believed you were too shy to attract a partner, your new belief could be, "My perfect partner will love my shyness. In fact, that one trait will attract him or her to me quickly." Imagine what that new belief would do — give you confidence, make you recognize that you are wonderful just the way you are. How do you act when you believe that you are wonderful? Shy? Please note that you do not change your innate quality of shyness. Instead, you change the belief that shyness is a deficit.

Let's take this a step further. In *Pygmalion in the Classroom*, Robert Rosenthal's and Lenore Jacobson's work with the self-fulfilling prophecy, proved that whatever you believe to be true sets up an expectation that actually impacts not only your own success or failure, but also the actions of those individuals around you. To illustrate this idea, imagine a man who says he wants his perfect mate and then sets out to find her. During the course of his daily life, he works in an office predominated by women; which could be delightful. However, whenever he has an occasion to relate with any of these women, he finds this one boring, that one bossy, the other an air-head.

The classic question is, "What comes first, the chicken or the egg?" In other words, are the women really boring, bossy, and airy-fairy? Or do they act that way because of the man's expectation?

The answer is: thought always precedes action. Beliefs set up expectations that magnetize your attention so you see nothing else, experience nothing else except that which you believe to be true. You are blind to all other options. And those around you can respond in no other way. Thus, our beliefs can lead us into a vicious circle with no end. But when we see that it is our original belief causing the cycle, then we know it can be changed. Another way to look at the example of the man in the office is this. Instead of sowing the seeds of judgment and being what I call "a make-wrong machine," he could look for the good points in each person he meets. He would soon find his work environment pleasant, and filled with good friends. This change in attitude would alter his life dramatically, and he would soon find himself attracting women who respond to love rather than criticism.

BASICS OF THE LAW OF CAUSE AND EFFECT

"As a man sows, so shall he reap," is the biblical way of explaining the basic law of nature. "Everything produces after its own kind" or "Whatever you send out returns to you," and "What goes around comes around," are paraphrases of that same law.

In our lives, we produce with thought energized by feelings or attention. We build our lives from what we believe to be true about ourselves and others. Our beliefs are the cause, our life circumstances the effect

— never the opposite. Jack Boland, former minister of Unity of Today in Warren, Michigan, often said, "You want to know what you believe? Look out your eyeballs."

Beliefs Acted Upon = Life Circumstances

This is not always obvious, because the "effect" is usually visible, while the "cause" is not. Nonetheless, our relationships reveal what we believe to be true. Here is a list of a few of the cause-and-effects I have seen:

Therefore, if you want to see the source of the problems in your life, go and look in a mirror. There

Cause	Effect
A belief that I'm unlovable	no relationships
A belief that I'm not okay	nagging partners
A belief that I'm not worthy	abusive partners
A belief that love doesn't last	relationships end sadly

you will find both the cause and the solution of all your woes.

"Mind is the Master-power that moulds and makes,
And Man is Mind, and evermore he takes
The tool of Thought, and, shaping what he wills,
Brings forth a thousand joys, a thousand ills:
He thinks in secret, and it comes to pass:
Environment is but his looking-glass.
As a Man Thinketh by James Allen.

In the Bible, Jesus said, "Judge not by appearances," because appearances are the result or effect of belief, they are not the cause. We think in secret, but everything in our life attests to our beliefs. Is it that simple? Yes.

My own experience is proof of this law. The belief I found most difficult to change in myself was the feeling that I was worth less than those around me, and undeserving of true love and affection. This low self esteem drew to me partners and situations which reflected my core beliefs. I went from a boyfriend who thought it was okay to hit me, to a husband who married me to escape the draft. After ending that marriage, I began to date a man who drank and did drugs. I narrowly escaped being the entertainment at one of his parties, and swore off dating until I met someone entirely different, a college professor. Unfortunately, he wanted me to marry him so I could be a mother to his four children. Then I survived a brush with death on a beach in San Francisco, only to end up marrying an alcoholic. Whew!

Now, the unaware person might think I was just unlucky in love. But the important part for you to understand is that I kept getting into bad situations *because I didn't believe I deserved better.* And the reason it was so hard for me to change my negative beliefs is that *I was assigning blame, instead of looking within myself.*

Oh yes, first it was the men's fault. If those men had behaved differently, my life would have been better. (In retrospect, of course, the responsibility is clear: *I* am the only constant factor in all of the events of my life.) Then I began therapy, and counseling helped me to see that what I had learned during my childhood had impacted my ability to respond. So! I had finally found the guilty parties! It was because I had inherited my parents' low self esteem, that I was having so much difficulty. I promptly blamed everything on my parents and all those people in the past.

The turning point came when I finally realized my parents had done the very best they could with what they, themselves, knew. And I faced the truth: my choices, made moment-by-moment, had brought me to each event in my life. I, whether knowingly or unknowingly, had chosen every bit of it. As soon as I faced this fact, as soon as I changed my beliefs and made different choices, my experiences also began to change.

> "We evolve through suffering."
> Yogacharya Oliver Black

Likewise, when you review the previous example of the shy person with the knowledge of cause-and-effect, a whole new set of possibilities arise. The problem is not shyness. It is the person's belief that he is too shy to be attractive to the right person, which then causes him to act, and ignore the very situations that would lead to success. I would not recommend that he change from shy and retiring to outgoing and gregarious, that's pretending. Instead, the solution is to recognize that his shyness is a great attribute, and to go forward, confident that his perfect partner will recognize him because of it.

In my true story in the second section of this book, I relate how I found my perfect partner. One of the biggest lessons for me to learn was that, unless I was being myself, my partner would not be able to recognize me. For years, I had changed how I looked, acted, and thought to try to please the men in my life, to no avail. Then I recognized that my partner wasn't the problem. It was me. I had been attracting men into my life who liked the facade I presented. But that was not the true me. It was my feeling of unworthiness that caused me to believe I had to change. When I woke up and began to love myself, with all my warts and weaknesses, I found Rich. He was attracted to me **because** of who I am. In fact, he would have passed me right by, had I not been genuine. And the reason it was easy for him to accept me was because he loved himself.

HOW THE MIND WORKS

The importance of belief is presented in this verse from the Bible, "If thou canst believe, all things are possible to him that believeth." You may think this is a powerful statement, maybe even too good to be true. But, in fact, life is determined by what we believe.

Thoughts are powerless without feelings. But once they are combined and planted into the subconscious mind, the life circumstance that is inherent in the belief is made manifest.

THOUGHT + [FEELING or BELIEFS planted in the subconscious] = LIFE CIRCUMSTANCES

The three switches in the mind are:

- SUPER-CONSCIOUS
- CONSCIOUS
- SUBCONSCIOUS

The *conscious mind* is the part that receives signals from our five senses. Like a TV receiver, it does not discriminate regarding the quality or source of the information it receives. It just accepts whatever is offered. Therefore, everything you have ever heard, seen, felt, tasted, and touched — as well as everything you have thought, read, watched on TV or listened to on the internet or radio, has entered your awareness through your conscious mind.

The *super-conscious* is our intuition, our conscience, our observer. It has the power of discernment, and can distinguish that which is highest and best. It is the part of us which whispers minute instructions, can save us from danger, and even communicates through our body, most often, the heart and solar plexus. Unfortunately, most of us don not listen to its advice. Instead of filtering out false or unhealthy information, we allow all that comes through the conscious mind to be dumped right into our memory bank, the subconscious mind.

The *subconscious* is the part of our mind which stores all our experiences, thoughts, and beliefs as memories. It is also the part which acts upon our beliefs, both running the body and creating our life circumstances according to them. It is like the soil in our garden. It accepts whatever seeds it is given and brings forth the plant. It will grow weeds, flowers, vegetables, whatever. **It is incapable of doing otherwise. It has no power of its own. It can only grow the seeds it is given.** Therefore, if we are unhappy about our life experiences, we need to go into our **subconscious mind** and weed out the beliefs that are causing us pain.

Another way of explaining this is to compare our mind to the way a computer operates. The Conscious mind is the keyboard, and the Super-conscious mind is the operator, while the Subconscious mind is the long-term memory. The keyboard has no way of screening out inaccurate data. The memory will store all data, even if false. All the calculations the computer performs and the results it produces are based upon the data it receives, as entered, regardless of its validity. Garbage In = Garbage Out

To correct the computer's output, the operator must locate the errors, change the data, and reprogram its memory. So it is with our minds. We must reprogram our beliefs. We must change our thoughts and feelings.

How Choices are Made

Decision-making begins when a piece of information is presented to the conscious mind. Now remember, the conscious mind is only the keyboard, or the receiver of the information. In the ideal situation, the conscious mind passes the perceived information on, to the super-conscious. After all, the best decision can only be made by the super-conscious mind, the operator. If the super-conscious mind deems the information healthy, productive, and useful, it is then acted upon and sent to the subconscious for storage. Otherwise, the information is discarded.

The situation for many people is very different. If we are not paying proper attention when a choice arises, the question bypasses the super-conscious filtration system and goes directly into the subconscious memory bank for comparison and analysis. This is where the problem lies. While the super-conscious is able to make valid decisions based upon the here-and-now, the subconscious only has access to the outdated information stored in its memory banks. Therefore, the subconscious mind is incapable of making a *new* decision. Only the super-conscious mind can filter the incoming data for accuracy and validity, determining whether a new course of action is required.

People get caught in ruts, repeating the same mistake over and over, when they operate on automatic pilot, allowing their negative programming in the subconscious to govern their decision-making. Only when we are aware, when we pass new information through the filter of our super-conscious, are we able to make the best choices. When we follow our intuition, we are guided to our best course of action through our soul.

In my own experience, all the men I picked made my second husband, M, look like a prince because I kept relying on my conscious and subconscious mind. When I began to use my super-conscious mind, through my intuition, I met Richard. Only then was I able to bypass my legacy and all the error-filled data in my memory bank.

HOW TO CHANGE BELIEFS

"Be ye transformed by the renewing of your mind." This verse from the Bible shows the critical relationship between our lives and our minds. Your life won't change until you change the way you think and feel, what you believe. And what you believe is most obvious in the quality of your thoughts, words, and actions.

The first step in changing your beliefs is to become aware of your inner dialogue. Pay attention to the thoughts you entertain. Set aside a few minutes each day to become quiet and watch your mind. Learning to meditate will greatly help you to become quiet. Attention is one of the great secrets of successful living, because even focusing on someone else's faults reinforces those same negative habits in your subconscious mind.

"Every idle word that men shall speak, they shall give account thereof in the day of judgment, for by thy words thou shalt be justified, and by thy words thou shalt be condemned."

Many individuals believe that the above statement from the Bible refers to judgment in some after-world. The truth is, we are judged by our words right now. In fact, our words have a powerful influence on our lives every day.

Words are thoughts spoken out loud. Each word carries with it a representative energy which is aligned with its meaning. The words that one speaks actually leave an imprint of the positive or negative energy they contain on the speaker. That is why words have the power to hurt or uplift, not only the listener, but the speaker as well.

If you listen to the types of words a person uses, you can tell the general nature of their life. You can also predict their future. Everyone is relieved when a "human skunk," a person who is crabby or fault-finding, leaves the room. By contrast, everyone is happy when a bright and cheerful person enters the room, so it is important to develop self-control in the words you use.

The second step in changing beliefs is to begin to watch the words you use. When you become aware of how you express yourself in thought and word, you can learn to flip the switch whenever a negative, limiting thought arises. This changing of consciousness is just as easy as erasing a mistake on a piece of paper.

METHODS TO ERASE NEGATIVE BELIEFS

AFFIRMATIONS are one of the easiest ways to weed negative beliefs out of your mind. Create a positive, current-moment statement about yourself, usually beginning with the words "I AM." For example, if your belief was *I don't deserve the right* <u>mate</u>, an affirmation to change that might be *I always deserve what is best for me, including the right partner.*

The best way to use affirmations is to repeat them with deep concentration and sincerity, upon awakening and just before bedtime. However, if a negative thought comes up during the day, flip the switch by repeating your affirmation. In this way, you erase the invading negative thought and replace it with your desire.

THE GOLDEN KEY By Emmet Fox. With this technique, every time a negative thought comes up, you replace it with thoughts of God, Higher Power, or Universal Truth. For example, the thought comes to you that you are <u>too shy to find your right mate</u>. You immediately respond by thinking about God, about His unconditional love, protection, mercy.

I remember when I first tried this technique. My mind seemed to be overwhelmed by negativity. I was living in Detroit at a grim time. There were gangs in all areas of town committing the most heinous of crimes. A person could not walk in broad daylight without carrying a baseball bat or some form of protection. Until I began to apply the principle of filling my mind with thoughts of God, I was nervous even when I visited my therapy group. If I heard heavy footsteps coming up the stairs, I would imagine it was a gang about to invade.

Often while driving to work on Southfield freeway the thought of a passing motorist shooting me would come to my mind. I would begin to think of my Higher Power and often actually screamed, ***"There's only one power in the universe and it is God and He is with me. There is nothing to fear."*** At first, the fearful thoughts persisted. After a few days, I noticed that the frequency had dropped off quite a bit, and after a few weeks of using the technique, they were few and far between.

Subsequently, I discovered these overwhelming negative thoughts had become lodged in my subconscious because I usually watched the news before bedtime. While I slept, my mind played the details of crimes over and over, imbedding them deep into my memory. Now it is rare that I watch or read the news at all. And when I do, I am always careful to read something uplifting and positive, as the last thing I do before bed.

BEAUTIFUL THOUGHTS This technique follows the injunction_*to think only that which is just and beautiful.* Again, the idea is the same: when a negative thought arises, replace it with the most beautiful thing you can think of. I actually ask myself, "What is the most beautiful thing I can think of right now?" Then I begin to muse on whatever beauty comes to my mind.

RECORDING Make a recording of your affirmations and listen to it while you jog, walk, bicycle, etc. Also, play it while you drift off to sleep. The subconscious mind is very vulnerable to reprogramming at that time.

BELIEVE THAT IT IS ALREADY DONE One of the most powerful ways to create a new life is to assume your wish has already been fulfilled. Many books have been written about the effectiveness of imagining what it would be like if your dream was already realized with Neville Goddard's writings among the best. Using this effortless way Neville suggests we get into a state of reverie, which is a quiet state of mind and imagine an experience that would indicate our new desire had been fulfilled. Richard confided that he would have dinner on Friday evening and imagine his partner sharing it with him. I made room in my house, in my closets and in my mind, preparing for his arrival. You can also imagine laying in each other's arms, the joy of your romance, or the sweetness of your love. Before Richard and I met, I would lull myself to sleep every night imagining myself lying in my partner's arms. I became so good at imagining what it would *feel like* to be lying in bed together that one night I actually thought someone had gotten into bed with me. The feeling was so real, I had to open my eyes to check. There was no one there, but it was as if I could feel my head on his chest.

And, it was shortly afterwards that we met. Again, there is a spiritual basis. "And whatever you pray, believe that it is already done for you." Ask yourself what life would be like if you already had your spiritual partner. Then imagine a scenario that would confirm your desire being fulfilled.

BLESS EVERYTHING When you are thankful for everything in your life, just the way it is, you set up a powerful vortex to draw more good to you. I reviewed my past and gave thanks for all my experiences, good and bad. The truth is, they were all necessary, and all part of my ripening process.

PRAYER AND MEDITATION Prayer is the request sent to God. Meditation is becoming silent, so you can hear the answer. The accomplishment of a quiet mind will work wonders in erasing negative beliefs.

QUICK AND WITH FUN I once believed life had to be painful and relationships required hard work. A friend pointed out that she always asked to learn her lessons quickly and with fun. I decided to try her idea and it has made all the difference. Whenever a problem arises or I begin experiencing pain, I simply ask inwardly, *"Show me the truth. Show me the good. Let me see the blessings and learn the lessons quickly and with fun."* It works miracles.

After the first printing of this book, I studied new modalities, over the next ten years, which quicken changes in our subconscious mind. These include: **Esoteric Healing, Radical Forgiveness and PSYCH-K**. I use these techniques in my work with clients and you may get more information by going to my website, www.karenabowen.com.

PRACTICE

Write down your current beliefs about relationships. Do you believe all women take advantage of you? All men are losers? All the good ones are married? Be honest with yourself. Make sure you get down to the core beliefs you hold, which determine the actions you take. If you really don't believe there is such a thing as a perfect partner, you need to do some reprogramming. Select one of the previous techniques that appeals to you and use it for 21 days. If you made progress using the technique, continue. If you did not, then use another one.

SECOND KEY

You must Believe it Is Possible for You to Find Your Perfect Partner

First, work with the basic law of nature

* If you want love, you must give love
* Focus only on that which you truly want in your life
* *Realize that what you send to another must come back to you. Then, operate the switches in your mind
* Pay attention to your thoughts and words
* Weed out negative beliefs and replace with positive
* Expect to get your lessons quickly and with fun

Affirmation

I now release all negative beliefs that have kept my true love from me.

*"Life is great
if you don't weaken."*

Yogacharya Oliver Black

Chapter Four

COMMITMENT

The THIRD KEY is: *You must Be Committed to Finding Your Perfect Partner.*

Sometimes we confuse commitment with intention. *Intention* is *"something I would like to do."* Contrast this with *commitment*, which means *"something I will do."* To me the terms "would like to" and "try" are both namby-pamby. If someone tells me they would like to or they tried, red flags go up all over the place, since I know the difference between those words and the definitive, "I will." In fact, if someone says, "I will try to be on time for our appointment," I know they lack commitment. I immediately ask, "Are you going to, or not?" It is like "trying" to drop a pencil you are holding. You either do it or you don't. There is no such thing as "try."

That reminds me of another term that some people confuse with commitment: the term "involvement." I used this explanation when I was teaching employee involvement in the auto industry. The difference between involvement and commitment is like the relationship a chicken and a pig have to a breakfast of ham and eggs. The chicken is involved; the pig is committed.

I repeat: You must be *committed* to finding your perfect partner!

COMMITMENT + ACTION = RESULTS

Each part of the above equation tells us about the quality of our commitment. If your commitment is weak, you will take ineffective or incorrect action, which will lead to poor results. By looking at the results in our lives, we learn about the quality of our action and the determination behind our commitment. We can also see what our TRUE GOAL was. What do I mean by that? Well, I have seen many individuals who tell me they want the right person, then marry someone who is not right for them. Therefore, to me, their true goal was to marry the wrong person. You see, I agree with Ralph Waldo Emerson, "What a man does speaks so loud I can't hear a word he says." The truth is, we are all totally successful in our lives, for we have achieved exactly what we were willing to pursue.

For example, a man who attended our workshop acknowledged that he wanted his perfect partner because he had a long history of bad relationships. Shortly after our workshop, he was again involved with someone he knew was not right for him. We had come to know him personally, so I had occasion to ask him why. He said, "I didn't think it would hurt." I responded, "Do you seriously believe your perfect partner is going to come looking for you in someone else's bedroom?" Falling into bed with everyone who gives you a smile means you have only made a commitment to having lots of sexual contacts.

If your past relationships were less than desirable, when you think back and analyze them you will find that you settled for somewhat less than the right person. You let something: looks, or money, or an ability to dance, or fear, or your sense of unworthiness, or the right religion, or your desire for sex keep you from the right mate.

No Compromising

So the THIRD KEY is that *You must Be Committed to Finding Your Perfect Partner* and the first action for this principle is NO COMPROMISING. Let's look at Webster's definition of compromise: 1. a settlement in which each side gives up some demands or makes concessions; 2. an adjustment of opposing principles, systems, etc. by modifying some aspects of each; 3. something midway between two other things; 4. to lay open to danger, suspicion or disrepute.

Often, individuals think compromise is good in relationships. I personally believe it can be a relationship's downfall, because compromise requires each person to give up something they truly believe in. How can you then be true to yourself? In my second marriage, everything was a compromise and neither of us was ever happy, because neither of us got exactly what we wanted. A friend of mine who is a psychologist once told me that compromise in a relationship goes like this: "You want to go to Florida and he wants to go to California, so you compromise and go to Iowa." Does not sound like much fun to me.

I believe compromise is similar to my method of keeping our dog and cat in the yard. I tie the ends of their leashes together, because they can never agree to go in the same direction at the same time. If you are in a relationship that requires compromise for harmony and stability, I would venture to say you are in the wrong one and that neither of you is going to get anywhere by always giving up what you believe in.

I have discovered that finding and keeping true love is not a matter of compromise. It is, instead, the result of being true to yourself. In our relationship, we take turns. Each Thursday we have a dinner date; we take turns picking out the restaurant. On weekends, we alternate the responsibility of activity planning. In this way, we both get to do what we really love, and we both expand our horizons. Now the truth is, as perfect partners, there is never a problem with the choices because, inherent in what we do, is the desire to always love and care for one another and to remain sweethearts. And I must admit, most often it is Richard who takes us to the more romantic places.

By being true to yourself, you can be true to your partner. Then no compromises need to be made.

JUST SAY "NO" GRACIOUSLY

A woman who attended our workshop decided to follow up with private counseling. During that time, she experienced several relationships which seemed designed to enable her to overcome negative memories of her father. Then she met the person she felt was her perfect partner. However, he was always too busy. With a business and children from a previous marriage to take care of, he just was not ready to make a commitment. After several months, she realized they were going in two different directions and broke off the relationship; she had promised not to settle for less than her perfect partner. Later she learned that he had met and married someone else. The problem had not been his busy schedule or not wanting to make a commitment. Rather, he had known their relationship was not right, but was unable to say "No."

Second action is: You must be willing to say "no" to those who are not perfect and LEARN TO SAY "NO" GRACIOUSLY.

Picture this. You are standing on the corner waiting for the bus. It is a simple thing to do. You do it every day. But today your bus is late. Others have come and gone. You remain patient at first, but now the frustration is beginning to show around the edges. After all, how late can a bus be? Finally, at your wits' end, exhausted with the wait, you board the very next bus.

As you climb aboard, you look at the driver and shake your head. No, it is not the bus you want. But it is a bus. You find a seat and fall into it. You have been standing a long time, and even the beat-up old vinyl cushion feels good. You decide to enjoy the ride for a while, then figure out a plan of attack. You have never passed this way before, so you are entertained by the fresh scenery and new faces, as people come and go.

Now, it is getting late, and you want to go home. You begin to complain to the person next to you about your late bus, and explain that you just got on board this one to take a breather. Soon, you are swapping "bad bus" stories with everyone around you. Next, you ask your new friends for directions home. Every idea is a loser. You know these people do not know. How can they? They have never been on your side of town.

Finally, annoyed and exasperated, you approach the driver with your story. He shrugs his shoulders, which ignites a plume of anger in you. After telling him exactly what you think of the bus company's inability to meet schedules and his insensitivity to your problem, a masterpiece idea strikes you. It is the end of the shift, why not have the driver take a detour into your neighborhood?

Without turning his head, a wry smirk appears on his lips as he says, "Are you nuts?" As you continue to berate him and expound upon the responsibility of the bus company in aiding you to reach your destination, the driver's ire begins to peak. At the next stop, he rises out of his seat and points to the door. Your joyride is over.

Now, I can hear you saying, "Who would ever do such a silly thing as knowingly get on the wrong bus?"

My guess, "About fifty percent of the people who get into relationships."

Every individual who has ever come for counseling or to our workshops has admitted, in some form, "I knew it wasn't the right relationship. But I thought we could work it out." Or, "I thought my love would change him/her." Or, "We had so much going for us, until..."

"What?" I ask. "What could you possibly have going for you when you are in the wrong relationship? How can you possibly get to the right destination by going in the wrong direction?"

The parallels are simple. You get into a relationship that you "know" is less than the best one and, shortly thereafter, you are trying to change your partner. Or you begin to complain, "If you love me ." "We never get to do what I like." "We always spend time with your friends." "I cannot talk to you, you won't listen." "You are always nagging me." "All you want is sex." Or, worse yet, like the wrong bus, you begin to compare stories with friends and acquaintances. Soon, everyone thinks relationships are full of pain and suffering.

Wrong! Why blame relationships in general, or even the other person specifically when *you* got on the wrong bus? Why ask the other person to become someone that they are not? It is your fault! You got into the wrong relationship. And all the work in the world cannot make the wrong relationship right.

It is like buying a suit that is too tight, and then complaining about the fit.

Why not recognize your error and get out of the relationship? Get off the bus. Or better yet, don't even get on.

One friend I have called me about the new guy she had met. After a few minutes of conversation, she admitted, "The only problem is that he smokes and drinks." My immediate response was, "Well then, you do not have to waste any time with him." But she did. Even though she is in recovery and knows that users are not good for her to be with, she wanted a relationship so much that she was willing to go against her own welfare. It took a few weeks, but soon she realized that his handling problems with alcohol was a sign of much deeper problems, and she bailed out. The truth is, she knew from the "git go" that it was wrong.

Another individual wanted to find her perfect partner and get married. When she told me about the man she was dating, she offhandedly commented, "But he doesn't want to get married." Well, no reason to wait around to see if he changes his mind. Trust the words you hear, and run like heck.

One of the men who came for counseling told me of a wonderful woman he met at work. He was in the process of a difficult divorce and appreciated the flirtations they experienced. However, the woman had made it clear: she did not want to become involved. She was separated, and "didn't need more grief," as she put it. Still, he hung on to the possibility, and was offering to do work at her condo, take her for motorcycle rides, and generally do whatever he could to keep the relationship alive. Excuse me, what is wrong with this picture?

My final example of "Wrong Bus" relationships concerns dating a married individual. A client was dating a married woman. I asked why. Of course, I was told all the horror stories of how bad her marriage was.

"Why doesn't she get a divorce?" was my next question.

I was then told all the reasons why it was impossible at this time. The problem is, this client actually believed the woman would be true to him once she got a divorce. He believed she would honor her commitment to him, even though she had not honored her commitment in her last love relationship. I hope I am wrong, because "I told you so" is not in my repertoire.

Let me finish this section by making one last comparison. Trying to change another person is like thinking Bob Dylan needs singing lessons — why spoil genius?

The second part of saying "no" is learning how to be assertive. When I was searching for my perfect partner, numerous occasions arose where I had to practice saying "no" graciously. I would agree to go to lunch, and halfway through the meal, recognize I was with the wrong person. It took practice, but I learned to say something kind, "I had a very pleasant lunch and it was wonderful hearing of your _____, but I am uncomfortable with continuing our acquaintance. I wish you all the best in your _____."

I had to practice being definite and I had to remove ambivalent words from my vocabulary. The subject of being assertive is too vast to cover in a chapter. Locate a copy of *When I Say No I Feel Guilty* and practice the techniques offered in it. It will be well worth the few dollars of expense.

There is a perfect mate for you, if that is what you want. Actually, it is easier to find the perfect mate than it is to put up with mediocre, sad, and unfulfilling matches. Finding the right person can be compared, in a way, to selecting the right suit. You go to a store, look at the rack of clothes, and select only a few that appeal to you. In the dressing room, you find out which ones are too tight or do not fit quite right, and you put them aside. The right suit is perfect in every way. You are comfortable in it, and you always look and feel good when you put it on.

The same holds true in finding the right person. You may look at a lot of individuals; you may try on a few. But the right one will be perfect in every way. Now, what do I mean by perfect? The one who fits you perfectly, not a perfected person.

When you meet someone new, the best way to find out if you should spend time with that individual is to just say to yourself, "I want to see the truth about this person. If there is a lesson to be learned, let me get it quickly and with fun. But I do not want anyone but my perfect partner." In that way, you remain open and receptive. At the same time, you are clearly unwilling to get into something that is not highest and best for you.

Learn from each person that comes into your life, but never settle for mediocrity. The one who is perfect for you will fit you in every way! **You will feel comfortable, in harmony, at home.**

BE PERSISTENT — NEVER GIVE UP

The third action in commitment is: BE PERSISTENT — NEVER GIVE UP

How do we reach any goal? How did you get where you are today? Persistence.

As an example, follow the progress of one who aspires to become a doctor. As soon as the goal is set, obstacles arise. First, the right courses must be passed in high school, with a high enough grade point average to be accepted in college. Then, the means must be available to attend college to prepare for medical school. There are distractions all along the way. High school friends want you to go out with them in the evening and on weekends. They think you take studying too seriously. Your parents have chores for you to do after school. Then, there is the sweetheart who wants your time. If you make it to college, you may have the added burden of supporting yourself and paying your tuition. Exhaustion, frustration, failed exams, peer pressure, and financial burdens all test your determination. To reach graduation, you must overcome a great deal.

In fact, any of these obstacles or distractions could have taken the aspirant off track. In the end, success is won by the individual who persists. It takes day-to-day effort to remain undaunted. It takes ever renewing commitment to one's goal. Every time an obstacle appears, every time a failure occurs, the aspirant must continue, despite all odds.

This is what is required in finding your perfect partner. You must never, ever quit. After all, he or she is looking for you, too, waiting just for you.

"Success is won by the individual
who persists.
It is not the setting of the goal
that brings the prize.
It is renewing one's commitment every time
an obstacle appears,
every time a failure occurs."

SEX

It seems appropriate to talk about sex along with commitment. Sex has become "the most popular indoor sport," as Yogacharya Oliver referred to it. It is used to sell beer, cars, clothes, and internet service, as well as bathing suits and magazines. Sex seems to have mass appeal, so we need to talk about sex as it relates to finding your perfect partner.

Sexual activity seems to have four levels: violence (both mental and physical), sport or play, procreation, and love. When you make a commitment to find your perfect partner, you are asking for a relationship beyond the normal cultural experience. You are asking for what I call a Higher Love. You are, in effect, telling the Universe, Nature, or God that you are weary of mundane and unfulfilling matches, that you want something different. With that desire, comes the reality that you must go about seeking this special relationship differently, as we have been discussing. And sex is not separate from the other aspects.

The sexual experience between perfect partners is a commingling of body, mind and soul, in an expression of their love. Therefore, there is no room for anything less than loving and kind behavior. You will find that when you meet your partner, your deepest sexual desires will also be fulfilled.

But what about handling sex in the "looking for my perfect partner" stage? Very simply, if it is not your perfect partner, there is no need for sex. Strong statement? Yes. I have seen people get involved sexually, move in together, and live as partners without commitment. To me, that is a big mistake because sex clouds the issue. Ask yourself, "How can I share one of the most sacred parts of my body, as well as my experience, with someone I do not even want to be committed to?"

A woman talked about how uncomfortable she was discussing finances with her live-in boyfriend. She feels she does not know him well enough to discuss money. How ludicrous. If she does not know him well enough to talk about money, why would she share her bed? For the same reason that individuals will get naked, share intimate parts of their body, and even make a baby, but not make a commitment? Our culture has abandoned wedding nights and honeymoons as special experiences. We have relinquished the sacredness of parenting, family and sexual intimacy. To have a different kind of relationship, a perfect partnership, a higher love, sexual intimacy must regain its sweetness. To have your perfect partner, you must be more committed to virtues than to passions.

Yes, when I talk about making a commitment to finding your perfect partner and making no compromises, I mean that your whole anatomy is part of that commitment. Understood?

THIRD KEY

You Must be Committed to Finding Your Perfect Partner

* *Make No Compromises
* Be willing to say "No" to those who are not Perfect and Learn to Say "No" Graciously
* Be Persistent, Never Quit

A Prayer for My Perfect Partner

*O Eternal One,
I want only the partner that You have chosen for
me.*

49

To forgive and forget is a sign

of great strength and wisdom.

For, what you refuse to give another,

you cannot have for yourself.

Chapter Five

The **FOURTH KEY** is: *Wipe the Slate Clean with Introspection and Forgiveness*. In my workshops, I use a white board and large pads of paper to write down comments from the audience. At the beginning of this topic, I ask questions of the participants and write their answers right over top of notes already on the board. Sometimes the crowd lets me get away with it for two or three questions. Then someone usually bails me out by saying they cannot read what I am writing because of the underlying words.

The same thing is true in our lives. You cannot have a wonderful today if you are unwilling to let go of the awful past. It is like building a house where once a ramshackle tenement stood. If you simply backfill over the trash, your foundation will be on shaky ground. You will never know when some derelict part from the past will surface to scourge the present. You have to clear away the rubble and level the ground before new construction can begin. Forgiveness is the bulldozer that will remove even the most twisted, gnarled piece of debris from the past.

INTROSPECTION

"The Unexamined life is not worth living."
Socrates

Many of us are good at looking back at the past, but to really profit from memories, we must use them properly. Our memories can be a literal gold mine or a garbage dump. It is all up to us. To grow and change, we must analyze where we have been and how we got there. Then we must be prepared to take the necessary steps to work toward change. We must be willing to examine our lives with the desire to see the truth, and to recognize the things that are not working right. **In introspection, we must be willing to look within ourselves, into our own thoughts and feelings, to see how we took part in both the failures and successes of our lives.** In this way, we use the raw materials of our past memories to forge a new, golden future.

Unfortunately, most of us rehash the past, brooding over what was and what was not. We blame our parents, our education, our spouses or our lovers. We blame what happened to us when we were three years old, or thirteen. We see everyone and every event as responsible, except ourselves. In this way, we trash our past and never learn from it. Instead, we keep repeating the same mistakes. Not only do we keep repeating the same mistakes, we perpetuate the negativity, imbedding it even more deeply into our subconscious mind. The right use of memory is to learn and benefit from the past, then forget and forge ahead.

The majority of individuals believe that life on our planet is iffy, at best, subject to chance, luck, random acts of violence, which political party is in power, and the value of stocks on the exchange. In contrast, my experience has proven to me that life proceeds in an orderly manner, based upon laws that anyone can learn and master. We have seen how three of those inner laws operate: how desires determine our course in life, how beliefs affect whether or not we are successful, and how commitment guarantees results. However, I have found that even when all three of these ideas are absorbed and utilized, one can still fail. One can feel stymied, stuck, as if, regardless of effort, no progress is made.

WHY CHANGE THE PAST?

Peter, a friend from my days in the auto industry, once asked me, "Why would you want to change the past?" He posed this question at the end of a long distance telephone conversation so I never had the chance to adequately explain. But that is a good question, a very good question. Why would anyone want to change their past?

Your life at this moment is the sum total of all your experiences. Everything you have attained is a result of your past thoughts and feelings. Each of these past encounters left a mark on you, for good or ill. Happy experiences left a mark of love, joy, and peace — but the ordeals which were sad, negative, or ugly may have left a smudge of anger, hate, revenge, or resentment. To make progress in a new direction, you must be free to move, in order to change and grow. Positive energies from happy experiences offer strong footings that enable you to go forward with a light heart and build an enriching future. On the other hand, the smudges from painful trials are like a sticky goo that makes each succeeding step slippery, unsteady, and dangerous. And, at the same time binds you to the past, to the event and to the person. The more negative experiences you collect, the more you feel bogged down and glued to old thoughts and feelings, unable to grow and develop.

During one of our workshops, when we asked whether participants were interested in marrying again, one man responded, "Well I am not sure about that. I don't want to end up giving half of what I own to the person I dislike the most?" His statement was met by twitters of laughter from the group, until another gentleman offered this solution, "My first wife took me for all that I had, which was a lot. I would not do that again. I would have to have a prenuptial agreement."

In another group, a woman spoke of her desperate efforts to convince her husband to stop drinking. He was an executive with an insurance firm, who argued that he only used alcohol to wind down. He never remembered the violent outbursts or the humiliation of the children, nor was he interested in knowing how his drinking affected the family's finances. After twenty-five years of marriage, she got a divorce and moved out. Now she was dating a recovering alcoholic she had met at church.

Another woman explained that her first two husbands were emotionally unavailable to her; she had felt lonely and unloved. She was attending the workshop with her boyfriend, to determine whether they were meant for one another. However, she felt he never had enough time for her and that he did not want to be close in the ways that were important to her.

Another individual spoke disparagingly of his former spouse. He ridiculed her, saying "She does not have the sense to come in out of the cold." He complained that they had never done things together and concluded that the only good thing about their twelve-year marriage was his daughter.

Despite these seemingly different circumstances, there is a common ground these individuals share. They are all unaware of the impact their angry, resentful, or limiting memories have had on their present choices in relationships. This common frailty is one of the largest stumbling blocks to finding the ideal partner. How can you experience joy and happiness in the present moment when your mind is full of hate, revenge, disgust, loathing, and fear from the past? When you hold up the magnifying glass of painful memories to every new person you meet?

It is impossible. That is why changing the past is very important for anyone who wants to make progress or begin a new direction in life.

"We should be careful to get out of an experience only the wisdom that is in it, and stop there; lest we be like the cat that sits down on a hot stove lid. She will never sit down on a hot stove lid again and that is well; but also she will never sit down on a cold one anymore."

Mark Twain

So, how do you wipe the slate clean? **You must forgive every person who has ever harmed you**. Tall order? Yes, it is a very tall order. But when you see the change it makes in your life, you will know it was worth it.

Every negative experience you have stored in your memory ties you not only to the past, but also to the person. If you do not believe me, just recall one experience and feel the negative energy of anger, hate, remorse, and rage. If you feel any discomfort at all, you are hooked, because the feelings are in you. They are constricting *your* blood vessels. They are elevating *your* blood pressure. They are deepening the grooves of memory in *your* subconscious mind. The person you hate may be entirely unaware of your feelings. And your hate has no power over that person, unless he lets it. *You* have a ball and chain attached to you, regarding that situation.

People tell me, "If you knew what so-and-so did to me, you would understand why I can't forgive."

This type of response indicates a belief that forgiving someone lets them off the hook, that you somehow condone what the person did. No. By forgiving, you are only letting yourself off the hook, because you are the one who is attached. Forgiveness is not a weakness. Forgiveness is a power of limitless scope. To forgive does not mean you allow the person to repeat the transgression, nor does it mean you cannot prosecute individuals for wrongs they have done. And it does not mean you must become bosom buddies with the perpetrator.

The examples I used earlier concern individuals who have not let go of the trash from the past, memories that keep them stuck in unproductive thinking, so they keep attracting the same type of individuals into their lives. Most of us do not realize that the reason we draw the same type of person into our experience is twofold:

- We did not master the lesson the first person brought to us.
- We did not forgive and release that person.

The process of forgiveness is an important part of removing negative thoughts and feelings from the subconscious mind, so they cannot sprout and grow into a repeat of the past. Forgiveness actually erases the sting of an experience and can transform a painful past into one of freedom and awareness. Forgiveness acts as a cleanser to remove the dirt and grime from your mind, which was full of mold, mildew, and maggots.

If you take your mind away from the pain of the past experience for a moment, and look at it from another perspective, you may be able to see the wisdom behind forgiveness. In Chapter Three we talked about the law of cause and effect, of sowing and reaping. What you send out comes back to you in spades. When a person does something that harms another, who is to blame? The perpetrator. Why? Because he or she chose, with his or her own free will, to commit the act or to speak the word. Who will suffer the consequences of the act? The perpetrator. Because of the inexorable law: what you plant, you must also reap. Does it have anything to do with you? Not unless you make it so. Always remember that you live on a round planet, in a round universe, and everything returns to its source. Water, in the form of rain, falls from the sky, quenches the thirst of all life forms, gathers in the rivers, rushes toward the ocean, and is evaporated by the sun's heat to accumulate as a cloud full of rain.

Now if you believe in the law of cause and effect as karma, you can rationalize and say, "It was my karma." Which may be true. If it is, why not be relieved that the debt has been paid and you are free? The cancelled debt should offer even more reason to forgive, because any retaliation would simply restart the cycle. For, if it is true that what we send out comes back to us, forgiveness makes more sense than any possible type of revenge.

We must also remember that whatever we focus upon, we become. Therefore, forgiving others is a very selfish thing to do. And, I might add, it is very wise. Your lack of forgiveness is only hurting you. You think, by remembering the past pain, you will prevent it from happening again. But the truth is, you are causing it to happen by keeping the memory fresh in your mind. Remember you are the cause of all your life, no one else. If you are caught in a negative pattern, you keep attracting the same kind of person.

Holding negative memories is like imprisoning the person you hate in your mind. Negative emotions of hate and revenge offer you a feeling of power, but it is a false power. When you experience the power of forgiveness, you will know what real power is. Real power never enslaves anyone. Real power sets everyone free.

If you are currently in a painful relationship, or one that is not meeting your needs, there is a very effective solution. Affirm earnestly, "I want this relationship healed to the highest and best for all concerned." Every time you think of your relationship, use that affirmation. But be forewarned, adjustments will occur quickly and completely if you are sincere. In fact, if you are headed in the wrong direction, sometimes these adjustments may feel as though you are being turned around at 90 mph. It can be a jolting experience. But do not worry; no one will get hurt.

My 90 mph spin began while I was trying to resolve the conflicts in my second marriage. I heard about the method through *A Course in Miracles* study group, and decided to use the above affirmation as a prayer. Within six months, I was divorced, had sold my business, and had moved to Milwaukee where, within the first week, I met my perfect partner, had I the eyes and heart to recognize him.

FORGIVING SELF

Besides our desire to be free of the past, there is another reason for forgiveness. Often, when we are wronged, it is because we did not stay true to ourselves. We knew, within ourselves, that the situation was wrong or that we could not trust the individual, but we denied our feelings out of a desire for love and approval, out of a desire to appear cool, tough or smart. Perhaps we fooled ourselves into believing the situation was not really that bad or the person would change. Let me give you two examples:

From Frying Pan into the Fire

My first two marriages were my workshops for resolving the childhood drama of having an alcoholic father whom I adored until I was seven, and a martyred mother whom I could never quite figure out. There was a lesson I needed to learn, but I did not understand it from living at home with my parents, so the Universe gave me another opportunity.

My first marriage was the result of giving in to manipulation and guilt. In truth, I knew the marriage would be wrong, but I did not have the courage to be honest. I just did not want to let him down or hurt his feelings. My boyfriend did not like the idea that I wanted to go to college. He thought, at age 18, I should want to settle down and stay barefoot and pregnant for the next twenty years. I persisted in my desire for an education, and the next year I finally won the scholarship which helped me leave my neck of the woods. During my first year of college, all went well. Then he called me in Buffalo to say he would be drafted because he was single. My heart was torn by his pleas for help. All I had to do was marry him a couple years earlier than we had planned. He said we would be married "in name only," if I was concerned about getting pregnant. On and on he talked about how we could elope at Christmas break, and no one need ever know.

He cried, he cajoled, he wore me down.

We had heard we could drive to Hagerstown, Maryland, and get married without my parents' permission. I agreed as long as we got married by a

Lutheran minister. There was a hidden reason to my request. I had been raised in the Lutheran church, so I understood that the minister would be bound by tradition to have a private conference with each party, separately, before performing the marriage ceremony. During my private time with the minister, I intended to tell him the truth: that I really did not want to get married. I knew the minister would then refuse to perform the ceremony, and let me off the hook. There was no way, at age 20, that I could tell my boyfriend "no," especially in such dire circumstances. I could not bear to be responsible for him being drafted into the Army.

My best friend and her husband drove us across the state line, and we arrived at the church a few minutes early. Waiting in the lobby I felt pensive like a lamb about to be saved from the slaughter. Then the minister came rushing down the hallway, wringing his hands: he had an emergency, and we would have to waive the private sessions. My heart had not even had a chance to hit bottom before we were saying, "I do."

So I was married, at age twenty, to a man who wanted to escape the draft. Our divorce was final one month after our fourth anniversary. But I still had not gotten the lesson, so my education began anew with husband number two.

Four years after my first divorce, I met the most attractive man I had ever seen. He was in a recovery program, so I was sure any doubts about his sobriety would be assuaged. My second marriage lasted thirteen years and was filled with all the disappointment and heartache of trying to change an alcoholic. After it ended, I went about the process of forgiving my former mate for all the pain, but I still felt stuck. I knew, from my experience with AA, that being stuck is a symptom of a lack of forgiveness on my part. I searched my mind and heart for some experience I had not resolved, until one day it hit me that I had not forgiven myself. You see, part of me knew from the beginning that the relationship was wrong. There was another part of me, that ignored all the signs and warnings, that silenced my conscience, that lived a lie. When I finally forgave myself, I knew I was free. There was a "click" in my consciousness, an awareness that I did not have to repeat that particular lesson again.

Both of these men represented the father I was trying to heal, just as my mother had tried to save and change my dad, because her father had been an alcoholic. After forgiving myself, I knew I would never have to save any more "needy" men.

Prenuptial Agreement

The wealthy gentleman who attended our workshop and recommended prenuptial agreements did not understand that he has to let go of the past before he can have that right relationship, that beautiful partnership we are talking about. If he believes a prenuptial agreement will solve his problem he is deluding himself. A prenuptial agreement does not absolve anyone of making the right choice. Often, the unspoken message is, "I do not trust you. I do not think our love is going to last, and I need protection." Talk about a self-fulfilling prophecy! Better to reach the point where we can tell the wheat from the chaff, or come to the realization that believing all partners take advantage of you, will actually create that in your life. Do not blame the partners. You picked them, made to order. A healing is called for.

If he sincerely wants the right relationship, he will work through the forgiveness process. By doing this, he may be able to see his own part in the downfall of his twenty-two year marriage. He may even see that his wife's settlement was actually her fair share. While he was building his business empire, she was the support staff on the home front. She took care of the home, raised the kids, made his free time comfortable and relaxing, and generally enabled him to succeed.

He may also see that he does not need the insurance of a prenuptial agreement if he has found the right partner. If he is open and receptive, he will know when the relationship is right. His whole being will attest to the fact. And, in the same manner, he will know when the relationship is wrong. No prenuptial agreement can save us from ignoring what we know to be true. A necessary part of forgiveness is to see our part in attracting the wrong situation in the first place.

TWO PROCESSES OF FORGIVENESS

One of the benefits of forgiveness is seeing that everything and everyone in your past was perfect. Recognize that your parents did the very best they could, given their own upbringing and experience.

Understand, also, that your upbringing and choices caused you to attract individuals into your life who allowed you to recreate what you learned at home. But today is different. Today is the day you change your life, for good, forever. You take command of your own journey when you learn the lesson of forgiveness, for you decide what to keep in your treasure trove of memories. You decide what impact your memories will have on your life. As you apply this power, your life will never be the same.

#1 FORGIVING OTHERS

1. Write down the name of everyone who has ever hurt you in any way.
2. Find a time when you can be alone. Before bed time is especially good for this portion of the process. Start with the first name on your list and use one of these methods:
    a. Picture the person in your mind. With as much sincerity of heart as you can muster, say to that person, "I forgive you for all you have done. I bless you, I release you, and I set you free. You are free and I am free, forever."
    b. Find your own words to speak to the person in your mind, recalling what they did to cause you harm and saying you forgive them.

3. Go on to the next person.
4. When you are finished with your list B this may take hours, days, or weeks, as it did in my case B put the list away.
5. In two weeks, go back to the list and look at each name purposefully. Do you still feel a tinge of pain, anger, or hurt? If you do, send that person a blessing, then let it go. Later, if the situation or person returns to your mind simply say, AI bless you,≅ and again let it go.
6. Repeat the process until there is no more ill-will felt.
7. Ceremoniously burn the list.

If you cannot get over the pain with a particular individual, say to yourself: **show me the lesson that I am to get through this experience.** Then trust that you will be shown, in some way, what you need to know. Often, the reason we cannot let an experience or person go is because we believe we are to blame.

#2 FORGIVING YOURSELF

1. Make a list of all the things you have ever done to hurt yourself or others.
2. Begin with the first item on your list. Go to a mirror, look deep into your eyes and with all sincerity say to yourself, AI forgive you for this. I bless you, I release you, and I set you free.≅ If this brings up emotion, continue anyway. Allow yourself to feel the sadness of keeping

yourself in prison for so long. Then drop the charges and release it.

3. Repeat this process for each item until there is no more guilt, shame, or other negative emotions.

4. Burn the list.

5. Recognize that life does not have to be painful, and you do not have to be martyred. Ask inwardly that you get your lessons quickly and with fun.

If you feel that what you have done is unpardonable, consider this: If God forgives you, who are you not to? Or, what if life is just a school? What if every situation is for your continual evolvement? What if, in truth, you never die but simply move from one level of awareness to another? What if all of the individuals in your experience are really dear soul-friends who have agreed to play assorted parts for your growth and unfoldment? What if each situation is just a lesson upon which we are tested?

CHANGING THE PAST

Quite a few years ago, after I used these two processes of forgiveness, my life began to change in amazing and wonderful ways, so I thought I had freed myself from past pain and programming. Last year, however, as I was writing about a childhood experience, I recalled a situation I had previously forgotten. As the circumstances of my brush with death came pouring into my awareness, I could literally see everything in my mind's eye.

When I was eight years old, my cousin Janet and I were allowed to spend a week at Grandma Ora=s during the summer. Janet was three years older than I, and mean-spirited B especially toward me. (One day, Grandma Ora promised to take us for a pony ride when we finished our chores. Janet refused to do her work. She knew how much I loved ponies, and she knew I would do her work in addition to my own, just to get that pony ride. But when Grandma Ora caught me scrubbing the wrong porch, she punished me by not letting me go see the ponies. That was the type of relationship Janet and I and Grandma Ora had.)

Missing a pony ride is not fatal, but as we walked back from the city pool one day, Janet challenged me with a dare. Now, can you imagine an eight-year old like me, in this kind of relationship, taking a dare? Can you imagine an eight-year old girl trying to prove to her eleven-year-old cousin (and to herself) that she is just as brave, just as strong, just as courageous? Especially when the eleven-year-old cousin had her own room with a canopy bed, tailor-made clothes, piano lessons and even a doll with a cradle B while I slept on a cot crammed next to my brothers= bunk beds in our pantry-sized living room, wore hand-me-down clothes from Janet, and was forced to endure such taunts as, "That dress looked a lot better on me."

Yep, I took the dare. I walked over the hill next to the Ben Avon bridge, to look down at the rail road tracks 300 feet below. I got as close to the edge as I could. Then I fell. Suddenly, my toes were just four feet from the bluff's edge; it seemed that every breath moved me closer to a terrifying death. With outstretched arms overhead, I clawed my fingers into the earth, frantically searching for something to grab hold of. No shrubs, no rocks, no grass or roots. Amidst my sobs and tears, I cried out for help.

Three feet above me, safely perched on the only rock on the hillside, Janet was laughing. "Afraid, Crayola? Think you're gonna die?" Her mocking tone and the scornful nickname she used sent chills through my body. It was then I realized: she really didn't care that I was about to die. In fact, she seemed happy about the idea.

But it was no time for anger, and I had no means of getting even. My only thought was how to escape falling 300 feet to the railroad tracks below. I screamed again and again, "Help me. Pleeeease, won't someone help me?" But with every cry, loose rock moved me closer. Now, just a few inches from the edge, I gave up and began to sob.

Suddenly there were voices — grown-up, male voices. As two men appeared at the crest of the hill, I heard one of them say, "My God, the little one is going over if we don't get to her." They locked hands, forming a human chain, and cautiously moved towards me. Careful not to start the loose gravel moving under their feet, they bypassed Janet and the closest man stretched out his hand to me. In one powerful lunge, I was safe. The fifteen feet between life and death, which had seemed like miles, disappeared in a few swift moves.

Safely on the sidewalk, quivering with yet-fresh fear, I brushed the dirt from my pants and jersey as the men returned for Janet. They had heard my screams from a nearby service station, they said. Now they wanted our names so they could call our parents.

Before I could think about it, I was running over the Ben Avon bridge back to Avalon. I couldn't let Grandma Ora find out that I had almost died. How could I explain that I had gone down the embankment on Janet's dare? I never told anyone what happened that day. What good would it do? But Janet's icy glare made an impression that lasted several decades.

Yes, even in my mind's eye, I could see the hate, the jealousy, the absolute contempt she felt for me. I could also feel the terror of my own situation, pleading for help, begging to be rescued. Suddenly, I was jolted back into the here-and-now, and instantly, I knew what I had to do. I closed my eyes, and with all the fervor of my heart I prayed, "Lord I ask that you go back through the past and down through my subconscious mind and erase this pain forever. I ask that you do the same for Janet and that she also be freed." A feeling of joy swept over me, and I knew that my prayer had been answered. A few days later, I discovered that Janet had died of breast cancer several months earlier. Maybe that wave of joy had been her way of thanking me.

I choose to believe that the power of forgiveness can reach beyond the portals of this life, and I know that we can change our own pasts. But forgiveness is only a tool. It must be *used* to be effective. And, like any other tool, the best results are achieved when the work is done consciously, knowingly, and deliberately.

HOW TO CHANGE THE PAST

Recall the situation that was painful and pray that it be removed from your subconscious mind and memory forever.

QUESTIONS ABOUT FORGIVENESS

Do I have to be "pure" or totally free of all resentment and hate before my life changes?

No. But you have to be at least 51% free. In other words, your predominate energy must be positive.

Do I have to let the person who wronged me back into my life?

No. You don't have to like the person to send him or her love and forgiveness.

What if I just can't forgive a particular person?

That's like asking me if you can walk forward while your feet are caught in quicksand.

My mind keeps going over and over ideas of what I could do to get even with my ex.

Yes. Have you ever noticed how good your mind is at making you right and the other person wrong? How you can justify or rationalize just about anything? The intellect catalogs, while the heart feels. You know in your heart what is right and what is wrong. You just don't want to admit it. Tell your mind to be quiet, or simply move it to another, more pleasing topic.

If I forgive everyone once and for all will I be totally free?

If you stop judging, yes. But for most of us, forgiveness is a daily event. Even after you meet the perfect partner, you will find it necessary to practice forgiveness.

Forgiveness is a power, not just a word. Forgiveness will wipe the slate clean. Forgiveness will erase the error without a trace. Forgiveness will smash all the barriers that are keeping you from moving forward. Mastering forgiveness is required to pass the course. Using the law of forgiveness is one of the secrets of navigating successfully through the mine field of Earth's trials.

Fourth Key

Wipe the Slate Clean with
Introspection and Forgiveness
Introspection

* Look back at your past with the objective of seeing the truth
* Earnestly pray or affirm that the current relationship be healed for the highest and best

Forgiveness

* Forgive all those who have ever harmed you
* Forgive yourself for all the wrongs you have done and for all the things you allowed to happen

Change the Past

* Pray that the memory be removed from your subconscious mind

I bless you. I release you. I set you free.
I am free and you are free, for all eternity.

"To thine own self be true,
and it shall follow
as the night the day,
thou shalt be false to no man."

William Shakespeare

Chapter Six

Self Love

Your mind can't stand a vacuum any more than the Universe can. Therefore, when we have completed the process of wiping the slate clean with forgiveness, we must fill our minds and experience with something else — something we want.

Self-love is a healthy respect for the uniqueness of our being, a recognition that the Universe (uni-verse or one song) is incomplete unless you play your part. In Ralph Waldo Emerson's essay, Spiritual Laws, he states:

"I desire not to disgrace the soul. The fact that I am here certainly shows me that the soul had need of an organ here. Shall I not assume the post? Shall I skulk and dodge and duck with my unseasonable apologies and vain modesty and imagine my being here impertinent? ...that the soul did not know its own needs?"

Self-love is a respect for the Being that you are. Each of us has a definite purpose. And the truth is, you cannot love another unless you first love yourself. If you were taught self-denial as a child, it was by those who knew no better. How can you love me if you can't love yourself? How can you give me something you don't have?

STOP ACTING AGAINST YOUR SELF

Begin to recognize types of relationships that go against your true nature.

A young couple sit opposite each other in a booth at a Chinese restaurant. She is neatly dressed in a blouse and shorts, her hair pulled up to frame her full face. His unshaven face, beat-up jeans, and shabby tee-shirt cast a sharp contrast. He has just sent his order of sweet-and-sour chicken back, because it was too crispy. She points out that he always sends his food back after he has eaten half of it. "You're picky," she concludes.

He quickly retaliates. "What! You think I should eat something I don't like?" Despite his small frame, his voice is coarse and loud. It fills the restaurant.

She changes the subject of the conversation to their relationship. "How do you feel about us?" He squirms in his seat without replying. I can't see his face, so I may have missed a nonverbal answer. She continues, "What? Is there something wrong about me?"

"Well, yeah. I don't want to get mean, but I do have a few problems with you. Like, you still live with Mommy and Daddy. I mean, you're 23 years old, and you don't make enough money to be out on your own," he says sarcastically.

She stiffens and sits back, "What are you talking about? How can you have a problem with me living at home? You live with your grandparents!"

"That's different," he asserts and continues, "My grandparents don't pay my bills. Your parents do. Plus, I'm not rich like your Dad, and I can't afford to spoil you the way he does. I don't have $200 a week to spend on you."

"I am spoiled, but why should I complain because my parents give me things?"

"Well, there's another problem. You spend more time with your friends than you do with me. And you don't call me when you should."

Overhearing that conversation, which was too loud to silence, it was obvious to me that the young woman was not quite hearing what her boyfriend was saying. He was accusing her of exactly his own faults:

(a) Not making enough money to be on her own. *Neither did he.*

(b) Being spoiled. *He was the one who always sent his food back.*

(c) Not being independent. *She lived with her parents, but he lived with his grandparents.*

The sad part, for me, was listening to the young woman try to defend herself and convince him that she was okay. She was doing what I call "a sales job."

I wanted to say, "Run, run, run. He's a "make wrong machine" that will drive you nuts!" I recognized the situation, and I knew she was never going to be okay in his eyes, no matter what. She couldn't even see that he might be jealous of her. Her family loved her so much they gave her material presents, while he had to live with his grandparents, who offered him no financial assistance at all.

I recognized her situation because I, too, had lacked self-love. There was a time when I could not even walk out of the house without makeup on, because my appearance had been picked at so much. I actually thought I was ugly without my mask of cosmetics, until one day when I looked at my husband and realized he was perfectly fine without powder and foundation, lipstick, rouge, eye-shadow, mascara, and eyebrow pencil. Yet, he thought I should cover my natural beauty with that which comes out of a bottle. Suddenly a light went on. I went into the bathroom and cleaned off my face. I realized I had been accepting the idea that I was not okay, that I had to make up for something God had obviously missed when I was created. How ridiculous.

Now, I'm not saying we should walk around unshaven and ungroomed. I am saying that if you like to wear cosmetics, a toupee, or whatever because it's fun, fine. However, if you wear them because you believe you are not okay without them, you're in trouble.

The next example of a relationship that goes against one's true nature involves a man who was once my best friend. Tom and I had worked in the auto industry and raced cars together, as well as being kindred spirits. After I left Detroit, he married the woman he had been living with for a few years. When Rich and I visited the area several years later, we stopped by to see them at the new home they had built in an exclusive neighborhood. As we toured the home, I noticed that Tom's favorite toys — a sports car and an airplane — were now missing from his life, as was his cat, Blackie. In fact, we discovered the car and plane had been sold to buy some of the fine and expensive furniture which now graced his home. Looking more closely, I realized that none of Tom's cherished pieces of furniture or objects d'art had survived the move.

When I asked Tom what had happened to Blackie, his wife answered quickly that her grown children were allergic to cats. Later, I asked Tom when he would be buying another plane. Again his wife interrupted, ATom doesn't need a plane, now that he has a house to be proud of." But the house didn't look as if it belonged to Tom, at all. During the one-hour visit, Tom said a total of three sentences. I was so sad. My best friend, the man I had been in the trenches with, had died. His ghost sat across from me, in the splendor of a home he had paid for with his life.

These three examples are a minute representation of how we prostitute our real nature to get false love. I did what I needed, to find my perfect mate. The young woman from the restaurant, if she chooses, can find a man who thinks it's great that she has parents who love her, because he will want to do the same. As for my friend Tom, I now know that he gave up our friendship, along with the other things he cherished, for the woman he calls his wife. I pray with all my heart that there isn't a woman waiting at an airfield for him, a woman who would have loved flying with him, not only in his plane and his sports car, but in his life, as well.

Self-love means being your true self. It is of the utmost importance in finding your perfect mate, because your perfect mate won't even recognize you, unless you are being your natural self.

In Chapter Two, I confessed that it took me three years to throw out my checklist of what I thought my mate should be like. What I didn't tell you was that I also had a checklist which applied to me:

- Always be slim and trim, with athletically toned muscles.
- Always be dressed appealingly
- Always have a high-paying, high-visibility position
- Live in a penthouse apartment
- Drive an expensive sports car

At the time, I was an ego-based individual who thought my worth came from all the "stuff" I had, how I looked, and — especially — how others viewed me. The reason I had to give all that up is because it simply isn't true. You and I are worth more than all the money in the world. We are so powerful and so awesome that sometimes I shiver at the possibilities awaiting each of us. My minister, Yogacharya Oliver Black, once asked me, "What would you rather be: a millionaire with mansions and yachts, or a Master who can manifest an orange in his hand?"

The other reason I had to change from being an ego-based individual to an inner-based being is because that's how my Richie is. It was part of my process of evolving. It was also preparation for meeting my perfect spiritual partner. When we met, he didn't even notice that I lived in a penthouse apartment, and it was very clear that my Porsche would not even have raised an eyebrow.

In order to find your perfect partner, you have to have a good deal of self-love going for you. I love Whitney Houston's rendition of *The Greatest Love of All,* because that's what we have to do. How?

PROCESS FOR SELF-LOVE

1. Write down all of your good qualities, abilities and characteristics. Every day, read them over to yourself, preferably upon arising and before sleep.
2. Stand in front of the mirror, look deep into your eyes and say B with conviction, "I love you just the way you are."
3. BE YOURSELF. Stop pretending to be someone other than who you are. When you do things you really don't want to, you are practicing false advertising, so why be surprised when you get into the wrong relationship as a result?
4. Stop martyring yourself by doing things for others that you don't really want to do. Make up your mind that you aren't going to do anything that doesn't lead to your own happiness.
5. Look at your personal habits. Do you wear cosmetics to "make up" for physical traits you feel are unattractive? Do you always have to look "perfect" before going outside? Or do you do the reverse, purposely dressing in a slovenly way so no one will pay attention? IF YOU DO THESE THINGS BECAUSE OF LOW SELF-ESTEEM, YOU WILL ATTRACT SOMEONE WHO ONLY LIKES THE FACADE.
6. Start to focus upon the 90% of you that is wonderful.
7. Pay attention to the way you treat others. When you love yourself, being gentle with those around you is natural.

8. Stop separating your heart from the rest of your body. Don't do anything that goes against your heart, including — and especially — having sex with someone who is not your perfect partner. In my previous marriage, my partner would nag and criticize me, then later expect me to be responsive to his sexual advances. Tolerating sexual relations out of a sense of duty is not an expression of love.
9. Remember: unscrupulous individuals won't care, but someone who truly loves you would never ask you to give up your beliefs or go against your heart.

Loving yourself just the way you are does not mean you will not make necessary improvements. On the contrary, when you love yourself, change comes easily and more rapidly.

WHEN YOU FILL YOUR SUBCONSCIOUS MIND WITH LOVING THOUGHTS, YOU DRAW TO YOU THE EXPERIENCES THAT MATCH THOSE THOUGHTS. It is impossible to find true love if you hate yourself B you can't give something you don't have. *If you hate yourself, you can only attract those who hate!*

FIFTH KEY
Love Your Self Just the Way You Are

* *Acknowledge your good qualities and characteristics
* *Be yourself
* *Do only that which makes you happy
* *Be gentle with yourself and others

Affirmation

I take a sacred vow to love, honor, and respect the unique being that I am.

I promise never to go against my true nature, for it is only by being true to my self that I will find true love.

*There are only two ways to live —
there is the path of wisdom. And then there is
the path of experience.
When you follow the path of wisdom:
you listen to your conscience or intuition
and follow the directions given,
or you learn from other's mistakes and
experience. In other words, you learn what works,
and bypass needless pain and unnecessary
heartache.*

*When you follow the long, arduous path of
experience: you ignore your conscience or intuition,
or you decide that the experience of others doesn't
apply to you — that what happened to them won't
happen to you — that you can beat the law. In other
words, you condemn yourself to learn the hard way
—*

*through failure, pain, heartache, and misery.
Which will you choose?*

Chapter Seven

Inner Wisdom

Gurdjieff, a great Russian philosopher, compared the human body to a horse-drawn carriage. If the driver (the intellect) was ignorant or drunk, he could take the carriage into a ditch. If the horses (our five senses) were unruly, they could take off on a wild frenzy and crash the carriage over a hillside. And so, Gurdjieff reasoned, the only one who should be in command of the care and destination of the carriage should be the passenger — our soul. Who is in charge of your life? Do your senses lead you around by the nose? Or does your intellect take you on a wild goose chase?

In Chapter Three, I explained that the best part of the mind to use for decision-making is the super-conscious. It is the part of the mind that can see around corners and through people, the part that knows when a piece of the puzzle is missing. It is the part of you that *knows* that it knows. In Chapter Four, I said that 90% of the people who get into relationships get into the wrong ones. To prevent further delay in finding your perfect partner the SIXTH KEY is: *Follow Your Built-In Guidance System, Intuition.*

Every moment of the day, your conscience is whispering to you, guiding you to the path you are to take. Are you listening? If you aren't, then don't blame your life circumstances on anyone but yourself. You have the power of choice, and you decide whether the unruly senses, the egoistic intellect, or the divine soul guides the ship of your life.

The Intuition is called by many names — conscience, the observer, higher self, "still, small voice," "infallible counsel of the inner voice," "wonder child." In Webster's Dictionary, it is defined as *the direct knowing or learning something without the conscious use of reasoning; immediate apprehension or understanding.* I believe it is our guidance system. Just as the animals have instincts and know when to migrate or hibernate, we have inner wisdom to protect us from harm and guide us to safety.

In *Spiritual Laws,* Ralph Waldo Emerson states, "There is a guidance for each of us, and by lowly listening we shall hear the right word."

This is the hidden meaning behind such sayings in the Bible as "The kingdom of God is within you" and "Seek ye first the kingdom of God and everything shall be added unto you."

We have all had experiences with our Intuition — times when we KNEW we were making a mistake, or we KNEW what was going to happen beforehand, or we KNEW something was wrong. I would like to share an example of the difficult lessons I needed to learn, concerning inner wisdom.

I became involved with a college professor. He was a widower 15 years my senior, who had four children. When I realized I was more interested in the kids than in him, I broke off our engagement. Calling off the wedding and saying goodbye to the children took quite an emotional toll. I was eager to get back into the dating scene and just have some fun, so my sister and I took a vacation to California. We jumped at the chance the first day at Fishermen's Wharf, when two "Hunk" cable car drivers asked us out. The guys didn't get off work until midnight, but that didn't faze us. The idea of getting a taste of the wild side of San Francisco was intriguing. Claudia and I were heading in two different directions, so I took the rental car to pick up my date.

Instead of touring exciting San Francisco night spots, my date and I ended up closing his favorite bar with a few drinks. A bit let-down and disappointed, but unwilling to offend him, I decided to be a good sport and pretend to enjoy his chitchat with the boys at the bar. Since he had missed his normal ride home, he asked if I could give him a lift. *It wasn't what I wanted to do (a nudge from my intuition), but I felt obliged.* As we drove along the bay, he suggested we take a stroll along the water. Was it the city lights, my desire to appear adventurous, my old programming of pleasing men, or just plain stupidity that had me walking with a stranger at 3:00 a.m.?

As we approached the water's edge, a terrifying feeling engulfed me. I felt as though I was in the presence of Evil, itself: I felt as if I was being strangled and smothered, although no one was touching me. Every hair on my body stood on end. Suddenly, I heard someone yell, "Run back to the car — NOW!" Without thinking, I ran at top speed. My bewildered date ran, too, and jumped in the passenger side. The instant I entered the car, I heard, "Start the car and leave now. And don't look at him." Only then did I realize that the yelling voice was inside me, and that "him" referred to my date.

As I drove at top speed, my date tried to get me to pull over, to look at him, or to explain my bizarre behavior. I don't recall what excuses I made, but I kept my eyes straight ahead, as I called out for directions to his house. Once there, I stopped the car in the middle of the boulevard, with the engine running. Again, he tried every conceivable ploy to convince me to pull over, look at him or get out of the car — including his desire for me to meet his mother, at 4:00 a.m., no less. Finally, unsuccessful, he left the car. As I drove away, the terrible evil feeling which had still surrounded me, left as well.

Claudia was waiting in our hotel room when I arrived around 5:00 a.m. I was still shaking with terror as I related my experience. Later, I realized that I didn't fully comprehend where the warning voice had come from, what the terrible feelings of strangulation and suffocation meant, or why I had felt so endangered. I only knew I was very happy to be in a safe place.

Years later, when I related this story to a psychologist, he told me, "That's the difference between a live lady and a dead one, Karen. We all have intuition, but we don't always listen. You did."

Over the years, I have heard many stories of intuition or a "gut feeling" being credited for saving individuals from death, crime, financial ruin, and heartache in the home. I have also heard instances of persons who didn't listen or who didn't have the courage to act upon what they knew to be true. I'm sure you have had experience with your own wonderful Counselor, but to find your perfect partner you must develop the ability — to receive and then follow guidance — to a keen degree.

When I began to consciously use my intuition, I decided to use it for small decisions first, so I could get a handle on exactly how it worked. I closed my eyes and asked, "What should I wear?" and I would see an outfit. While walking the dog, I would ask which direction to go. From these small beginnings, I advanced to receiving results that flabbergasted me.

For example, one day I asked for the best course of action, and I saw myself walking the dog. I was surprised, since the timing went against my normal routine, but I decided to trust the guidance. As I left my apartment, I noticed someone at the far end of the hall, near the elevators. He called out to me, "Do you want me to hold the door, or are you going to take the freight elevator?" I had seen myself going down in the main elevators, so I asked him to hold the door. When I got there, he greeted me warmly. I realized that he lived across the hall from me, but we had never been introduced. After the basic good-morning chatter, he asked what I did for a living. I explained that I was a consultant and did management training. He laughed and said, "Are you joking? I need a management trainer! What kind of training do you do?"

Within five minutes, outside the elevator, we had agreed to meet in his office that evening, to discuss my training 25 managers from his restaurant chain. The real joy was that I was unemployed at the time, and desperately in need of work.

Occasionally, a person attends a workshop who doesn't believe it is possible to be forewarned of danger. Think of it this way: if you were working as an air traffic controller, would it seem strange that you could predetermine each plane's exact location in relationship to the others, and that you could warn each pilot of potential problems? No. You would think that was normal. If you worked for the weather bureau and could map out the course of a storm, would you think it odd that you could predict which city would be hit first? No, that would be normal. We have built-in radar, our Asixth sense≅ or intuition, which can do the same for us B if we will use it. Here's another way of looking at it: the mind, which can create instruments to track storms and planes to receive sound and picture signals, must — by its own wisdom — be able to perform these feats itself. How else could it conceive to build such complicated machines?

The first rule of success is being in the right place at the right time. But how do you know when and where to be? Well, I am convinced that each one of us can do it, if we will only learn to trust the inner wisdom being offered. You may use any technique that appeals to you. The secret is to set up a system of communication with your inner wisdom that works best for you.

DEVELOPING YOUR INTUITION

1. Recall how intuition has worked previously in your life. Did you notice, for example, a feeling, a thought, a voice, a picture? Write down some examples of your experience. What happened when you listened to the hint that was given?

What happened when you didn't? Learn from your past. These memories will offer you a powerful bankroll that you can call upon over and over again. It is one thing to be ignorant, but only stupidity or hard-headedness causes us to ignore a warning twice.

2. Begin to use your intuition consciously — in other words, purposefully. Develop a stronger sense of it by using it to make small decisions. Ask very specific questions. Do you have inner vision? Letɔσ see. Close your eyes and think of the first house you lived in. Can you see it in your mind's eye? Or is it a feeling? Or a thought? Whichever it is, use these techniques to sharpen your awareness of your sixth sense.

   A. **Use inner vision:** For instance, if you want to go shopping, first ask yourself , "What is the best course of action? Where is the best place to shop for ____?" Then close your eyes, focus at the mid-spot between your eyebrows (the seat of soul intuition), clear your mind of any preconceived ideas, and relax. Whatever you see is the answer. If you see nothing, it means that shopping is not the best course of action at this time. Ask, "What is the best thing for me to do right now?" Close your eyes and repeat the process.

   B. Pay particular attention to your feelings in the solar plexus, (the pit of your stomach). This is where the "gut feelings" are felt. When you ask which is the best course of action, A or B, become aware of which one feels right.

"If it feels light and right, then do it.
If there is any doubt, don't."
Yogacharya Oliver Black

C. If you have a doubt about something, recognize that your intuition is probably warning you of a mistake or danger.

When I was first re-establishing my communication with my inner wisdom, I would offer it two choices. I would say, "If you want me to go to the store, show me which one. If you want me to do the laundry, show me the laundry room." One day, instead of seeing one of my two options, I saw a totally different inner picture. Voila! My intuition had a better idea. After that, I would simply ask, "What is highest and best for me to do right now?"

One day I got a phone call from a woman who wanted to meet for lunch. I couldn't think of any image to use with my inner vision, so I said inwardly, *I need a method of just knowing whether an answer is "yes" or "no."* Immediately my eyes, felt as though they were being pulled to the left. *Great,* I thought. *I will set up a system of communication whereby, if the answer is "no" my eyes are pulled to the left, and if the answer is "yes" they are pulled to the right.* I still use this technique, but the point is for you to establish your own, unique communication system.

D. Experiment with your own methods of using your intuition to answer "yes" or "no" questions. One person I know uses inner vision, seeing an eye which is either open or closed. Another uses a red or green light. One who is a masseuse uses the energy in her hands. She set up this communication with her intuition, "If the answer is "yes," let me feel energy in my right hand, if "no," send energy to my left hand."

E. Once you have established your own method, recognize that getting "no answer" means you should not do whatever you are contemplating.

F. If you receive confusing information, simply ask your intuition to make the answer very clear and understandable to you.

G. Trust you body's signals. If your neck gets stiff or your shoulders get tense, maybe you are headed in the wrong direction.

3. Do not rationalize, or try to figure out with your limited conscious mind, the instructions you receive through your intuition. In other words, don't let your ego get in the way, with its doubts and lack of understanding. Comparing your inner wisdom to your ego is like comparing an abacus to a computer!

4. Recognize that inner wisdom's direction is always PERFECT — especially when your intellect can't figure it out, or it is not logical.

5. Make a conscious decision to use your intuition for EVERY DECISION IN YOUR LIFE.

6. Ask only present-moment questions. Questions about the future, especially those involving other people, cannot be answered accurately. We all have free will, and many people choose not to listen to their intuition. That is their right, but it makes predictions unreliable because they may choose not to do what is highest and best. Also, if you ask a future question you begin to focus on expecting that result and forget to enjoy the eternal now. Even-mindedness is: enjoy what is, moment-to-moment. If you need future information, you will receive it.

7. DON'T GIVE YOUR POWER AWAY. Relying on astrology, psychics, doctors, psychiatrists, or any other system, weakens your ability to follow the perfect guidance for YOU — *YOUR* INTUITION. In fact, if anyone ever gives you advice, always confirm it with your own inner wisdom. If anyone, including myself, tells you they know what is better for you, *trust yourself.*

8. Command your intuition to direct you perfectly. **"Ask and ye shall receive."**

9. Trust the direction you receive, and practice until you can distinguish between your ego and intuition.

10. Strengthen your Intuition through prayer and meditation. Always pray by asking to be guided to the highest and best outcome for you. What is best for you must, by its nature, be best for all concerned. Meditate by clearing your mind and focusing your attention on God, your Higher

Power, Great Mystery, the Source, your own indwelling Christ. Become receptive, to receive the answer.

11. Strengthen your Intuition by following its guidance, especially in your heart. One area of particular concern is sex. Many of us think we can separate sex from love, but your heart knows you can't. Every time you ignore that truth, you harden yourself against your own inner wisdom. Soon, you will no longer hear its voice, for it never forces itself upon any of us. It must be a welcome part of our life. You must ask for and sincerely want your intuition's help. Don't deaden yourself. You can't separate your heart from anything you do. Don't try to fool yourself.

SIXTH KEY
Follow Your Built-In Guidance System, Intuition

* Recall how it has worked for you in the past
* Develop methods that you can use consciously and purposefully
* Ask for what you want

Thought to contemplate

"Humility is the key to power."
Yogacharya Oliver Black

Surrender is a letting go,
a releasing.
It is the knowledge that
what you earnestly desire
will come to you,
at the perfect time.
That you cannot miss what is truly
yours.
That the whole world works
together to bring about
your most cherished dreams.
And all is well.

Chapter Eight

SURRENDER

I know what you're thinking. You have already established a desire and believed it is possible. You are committed, and you've forgiven every yahoo you have ever known. You love yourself to the max, and follow your intuition perfectly. What else can there possibly be?

Well, let me give you a hint. What do you do after you've chosen the seed, planted it, watered it, and weeded the soil? You sit back and enjoy. You don't make the plant grow. You *can't* make the plant grow. You sit back and enjoy, knowing the plant will come forth.

> The **SEVENTH KEY** is: *Surrender to What Is Highest and Best for You.*

Many of us are afraid that if we surrender our desires, we will get something we really hate. This fear is usually based upon past ego-influenced experiences. But if you don't release your desire, how can it grow? If you hold it so tightly to yourself, it can't expand into manifestation.

My own point of surrender came when I realized that all my actions had resulted in failure. I earnestly prayed, "Heal me so that I may attract the one *You* have chosen for me. I want no other." I had come to the point where I wanted the right man, or no man at all. The next day, my intuition guided me to the place where I met Richard again, after three years. This time, I was almost ready to recognize him as my perfect spiritual partner. Only a few minor adjustments, "finishing touches" on my growth process, were needed before we could get together.

When you begin this journey, you may find your life changing in many ways. Instead of becoming frightened, you need to relax and have faith in the process. One of my friends calls this time "fruit basket turnover" because it can feel as if everything has spilled out of a basket, and you have to clean it all up. I like to think of it as Spring house-cleaning. When you are in the midst of the cleaning, everything is a wreck. Nothing is in the right place, there's dirt everywhere, and you're a mess. But when all the work is done ...Wow... I love a clean house and a changed life.

The truth is, if you are sincere in your desire to have the perfect partner, by its very nature your desire must be fulfilled. Which means there is someone just as eager to meet you, as you are him or her. I remember one conversation Rich and I had before I knew he was my perfect partner. He admitted that he had been looking for the right woman all his life, starting when he was a little boy. I didn't have to convince him of anything; he had had the same desire.

How do we go about releasing our heart's desire for the perfect partner?

First, by accepting what is. Most of the individuals who come to our workshops or counseling have the same problem I had: an unwillingness to accept relationships as they are. I had always tried to change the form of the relationship, and make it what I wanted it to be. I had refused to see what was staring me in the face, like the young woman who called me about her fiancée cheating on her, three weeks before their wedding date. If the man's heart is not hers now, how is a ceremony going to change that?

If you aren't 100% happy and bursting at the seams to be together, can it be love? If you don't look forward to spending the rest of eternity together — rich or poor, sick or well — can it be love? Look at your current relationship honestly. If it isn't the highest and best one for you, pray that it be healed in the highest and best way for all involved.

Then let go. Begin to live your life, being true to your self. Your higher Self.

THE PROCESS OF SURRENDERING

1. "Affirm: AI want the one tailor-made for me. I want no one else."
2. Release your desire for the right partner as if you are sending a carrier pigeon out with a message that must return, fulfilled.
3. Recognize that you do not have to *MAKE ANYTHING HAPPEN*. Change your thoughts, and your world will change.
4. Go about your life as though your dream has already been fulfilled. How would you feel if your perfect partner was already in your life? Act that way.
5. Recognize that there is no competition – the right one for you is yours alone.

6. Cherish your life and your experience so that everything becomes sacred.

SEVENTH KEY
Surrender to What is Highest and Best for You

* Accept what is, and let go of mediocrity
* Recognize that there is nothing to do
but be yourself
* You cannot make it happen
you can only prepare and let it happen
* It is not going to happen the way you think it should

but

* In the living of your life, you will meet,
  when you are both ripe
* And all the world will sing for Joy

Perfect partners are not only possible, they are our Divine Birthright and the way Love relationships are supposed to be. You no longer have any excuse. Go for it.

Summary

FIRST KEY
You Must Have a Heart's Desire for the Perfect Mate

* Give up all the items on your checklist.
* Become open and receptive.
* Expect your perfect partner to be more than you could ever dream possible

SECOND KEY
You must Believe it Is Possible for You to Find Your Perfect Partner

First, work with the basic law of nature

* If you want love, you must give love
* Focus only on that which you truly want in your life
* Realize that what you send to another must come back to you

Then, operate the switches in your mind

* Pay attention to your thoughts and words
* Weed out negative beliefs and replace with positive
* Expect to get your lessons quickly and with fun

THIRD KEY
You must Be Committed to Finding Your Perfect Partner

* Make No Compromises
* Be willing to say "No" to those who aren't Perfect and Learn to Say "No" Graciously
* Be Persistent, Never Quit

FOURTH KEY
Wipe the Slate Clean with Introspection and Forgiveness
Introspection

* Look back at your past with the objective of seeing the truth
* Earnestly pray or affirm that the current relationship be healed for the highest and best
* Forgiveness
* Forgive all those who have ever harmed you
* Forgive yourself for all the wrongs you have done and for all the things you allowed to happen
* Change the past
* Pray that the memory be removed from your subconscious mind

FIFTH KEY
Love Your Self Just the Way You Are

* Acknowledge your good qualities and characteristics
* Be yourself

* Do only that which makes you happy
* Be gentle with yourself and others

SIXTH KEY
Follow Your Built-In Guidance System, Intuition

* Recall how it has worked for you in the past
* Develop methods that you can use consciously and purposefully
* Ask for what you want

SEVENTH KEY
Surrender to What Is Highest and Best for You

* Accept what is, and let go of mediocrity
* Recognize that there is nothing to do but be yourself
* You cannot make it happen; you can only prepare and let it happen
* It is not going to happen the way you think it should – but
* In the living of your life, you will meet, when you are both ripe
* And all the world will sing for Joy

Part Two

A True Story

**HOW I FOUND
MY PERFECT MATE**

One rarely considers all the resistance that must be overcome, all the hardships that must be endured for one tiny blossom to unfold amidst the rocks. To open its petals and face the sun, unfettered, joyful and free at last.

Awakening to the Dream

It all began in Waikikii, during my first trip to Hawaii. I was attending a New Thought Convention, thoroughly enjoying the lectures and sightseeing experiences. During a break in the schedule, I wandered through the outer lobby of the luxurious hotel, admiring the beautiful marble fountains and palm trees. Through the open windows, a wonderful breeze carried a mellow excitement of warm chills that filled the room. As I browsed a nearby table filled with books for sale, my attention was drawn to a title that seemed quite different from the rest. *Beyond the Love Game* by Robert Scheid seemed almost frivolous beside the stately books on mind control and higher consciousness. My curiosity piqued, I picked up the book and leafed through it.

I had never in my life read a book about love; in fact, my training and personality were more the "nuts and bolts, scientific-type." Yet, I found myself handing the clerk money to purchase this intriguing book. Even more mysteriously, wherever I went for the rest of the day, I found myself hungrily stealing moments to read a few pages. Like an adolescent schoolgirl possessed by some fantasy and carried away on the winds of imagination, it was difficult for me to pay attention to anything else around me.

I was captivated by the idea that there are "perfect mates" for anyone who has this desire. I had never heard of such a thing. Certainly, I had heard people say, "There's a match made in heaven," or speak of "twin souls" and "soul mates," but I really did not believe in that sort of thing.

Since I had already been through one divorce and plenty of painful relationships even before my second marriage, I knew that male-female relationships were much less than perfect. I knew a lot of sacrifice and compromise were required. After all, here I was enjoying Hawaii while my second husband preferred to stay in Detroit and spend his vacation on our boat. My greatest successes in relating to men had been in friendship-only situations. In my love life, I always seemed to match myself up with guys who did not understand me or who did not care about me in quite the way I wanted them to.

The more I read Scheid's book, the more I cried. He described beautiful relationships, filled with fun, love, and harmony: relationships between equals, where mutual respect, cooperation, and kindness, as well as physical attraction and satisfaction, were the norm — all the things I had always wanted, but had never seemed able to find in my own experience. Here, for the first time in my memory, someone was saying not only that this kind of relationship was possible, but also that relationships were actually intended to bring all these things, in abundance.

I was hooked.
I made up my mind to someday
find my perfect mate.

Reality Re-enters

It was obvious to me that I had quite a bit of work to do before obtaining my goal. One major obstacle was my current marriage. The Schied's warning, not to hold any preconceived notions of who my perfect mate would be, was also particularly difficult for me to accept. How could I follow this author's directions, to be totally open to any possibilities when, after six very stormy years of marriage, I found even the suggestion that my current husband might be the "right man" a very bitter pill to swallow? Finally, as the days went by, I was willing to accept even this fate when I realized that if it were true, my marriage would eventually turn out to be wonderful and joyful; at least, as soon as we worked out all our differences.

One day, I noticed some sun suits in the window of a shop in Lahaina, Maui. My husband had made it quite clear over the years that the way I dressed greatly influenced our relationship, and his ardor for me in particular. If he was my perfect partner, I reasoned, I should dress the way he wants me to. So, into the store I ventured, although it never dawned on me that there might be something inherently wrong with the relationship, if I always had to dress seductively for him. I bought the skimpiest, sexiest outfits I could find, including a soft pink one that was gathered at the waist with just enough material to barely cover my cheeks at the bottom and to caress my breasts above. My body was golden from the Polynesian sun, and showed the tone of one accustomed to health-club workouts and high-energy aerobic drills.

Several days later, as I boarded the plane to return home, I wondered if HM would be at the airport to meet me. Just two weeks earlier, at my departure, he had angrily remarked that I could find my own way home when I returned from Hawaii. We had not spoken since.

I peered at the airport crowd in Detroit, but HM was nowhere to be seen. I was disappointed but not surprised. It would be inconvenient to get a cab and to lug the suitcases into the house by myself, but there was no real fear in the situation. As I continued to scan the crowd, I caught a glimpse of a very handsome Latino-looking gentleman who was leaning against a column. He wore a beautiful hand-painted shirt, left open to reveal his chest hair and gold chain. His snug-fitting slacks, Cuban-heeled shoes, and bold machismo posture all reminded me of my dream man — the one I had always hoped to meet — the one I imagined whenever I heard the song, "Some day my prince will come." Because he wore sunglasses, I couldn't tell if he had noticed me, but for just a moment I thought he might be admiring my new, very short tunic that revealed athletically sculpted legs. I had changed clothes on the plane, hoping to please HM and to help rekindle our relationship.

Suddenly, the man began walking toward me. In partial disbelief, unsure what to do about this unsolicited attention, I also felt excited that someone so attractive might be interested in me.

As he drew closer, I tried to gather my thoughts and prepare to handle this encounter, when suddenly I saw his eyes through the dark lenses. It was HM! Shocked and a little frightened, I felt as if I had been caught flirting with another man. At the same time, I was having trouble believing it was my husband. He had always been very handsome, oh yes, with an Adonis-type body, but never, ever, had I seen him dress this way.

Maybe I had been wrong, I thought. Maybe he *was* the perfect mate for me, and I had just been too blind to see. Maybe I really had been too selfish, as he had so often pointed out, always wanting things my way.

Someday, My Prince or
Looking for Love in All the Wrong Places

It had, of course, been HM's striking good looks which attracted me when we first met. I had dropped in on my friend Gary for a surprise visit, only to discover that he was about to host a party. It was just before his guests began arriving, and I accepted Gary's invitation to stay. When I first saw HM as he walked through the door, he looked magnificently like the prince I had long been seeking: well-chiseled features, matching physique, and dark brown hair cut in a Princeton.

We all sat on pillows around a coffee table topped with bowls of popcorn and little dishes of raw nuts and dried fruits. Bottles of soda and cups of herbal tea rimmed the table edge. The obvious lack of alcohol and drugs wasn't because we were prim and proper "straights." The fact was, everyone at the party, myself excluded, was in a recovery program.

As the evening progressed, I was particularly intrigued by HM's total disrespect for anything religious, and by his view that "If there was a God, he had certainly made a total mess of the universe, and of this planet, in particular." With my strong Christian upbringing, I decided to win him over to God's side. I argued each point with objective, tell-it-as-you-learned-in-Sunday-school logic. By the end of the party, we were alone in a secluded room that was usually used for meditation, although nothing happened except a few unsatisfying kisses. In retrospect, it felt as if I was coaxing him to come alive. As the crowd broke up, I invited HM to stop by my place in Dearborn the next day.

His visit wasn't a romantic rendezvous; he was withdrawn and reserved, and I found myself trying to cheer him up. He told me of his bout with alcoholism and his attempt to commit suicide, of his broken dreams and his shattered life. In keeping with the gloomy tone of his visit, he once looked around the room at the 30-odd trophies I had gathered for winning races with my Production Corvette and said, "Don't you know racing's hazardous for your health?"

I realize now that I had no idea what a healthy relationship looked like, because I did not even notice the obvious warning signs that should have triggered red flags and sent me running in the opposite direction. Instead, as we sat on the couch, he looked like a wounded prince in need of True Love, and I must have decided I was the one who could rescue him.

He had been in recovery only a few months before we met, but he seemed pretty healthy to me. I took lunches to him at the car wash where he worked by day, and he slept at a recovery half-way house each night. Although we truly lived in different worlds, to me we seemed compatible. By April, he had moved in.

HM's degree in economics did not seem to offer much employment potential. First, he tried his hand at real estate. He did not sell any houses, but he did prove he was a great salesman. When he explained that he couldn't be successful in real estate because he drove an old, dilapidated car - well, since I was working for a Detroit automotive firm, it just made sense for me to buy a fancy new car for him to use. So I did, although I felt very uncomfortable with the idea.

When he still couldn't make money selling houses, he decided to look for employment elsewhere. In autumn, he landed a sales job at a company which preferred married men, so he asked me to marry him. "What have you got to lose?" he said.

On November 5th we were married, and he celebrated by having a drink. In fact, he had several drinks. In fact, he got plastered. And, as he came out of the bathroom on our wedding night he announced to me that I was married, but he was not. The thought came to me, "Leave him now." (Could that have been my Guardian Angel whispering?) Quickly I countered that idea with, "What will people think if they find out I'm a two-time loser?" and "How can I just leave him?"

The remainder of our honeymoon trip was from one bar to another in our camper truck. At one point, he got so sick I had to take him to an emergency room. One would think, by this time, I would have had the sense to leave him with the doctors, go home, and get an annulment. In fact, that thought did arise.

If someone asked me today, "What do you have to lose?" I would tell them:

"I can lose my health, wealth, and peace of mind by doing something that isn't highest and best for me. No thanks."

Our first year together saw major events. HM shook off the drinking, for a time, and was promoted to sales manager of a territory, which included all of Missouri and part of Illinois. I was an engineer with Ford Motor Co. and couldn't get a transfer, so he flew home almost every weekend.

While things seemed to be going very well for him in his career, our relationship wasn't as successful. even without the drinking. Nothing I did seemed to please him. If I spent most of the weekend helping him with his paperwork, then I wasn't taking care of meal planning properly. He did not like the color of my hair, so I bleached it blonde. He said I laughed too loud, so I quit laughing. He thought women shouldn't tell so many jokes, so I quit joking. He preferred women who wore makeup, so I learned to apply cosmetics. He complained that my clothes weren't sexy enough, so I bought more appealing ones. He liked tennis and golf, so I took lessons. No matter what I did, it just never seemed to be enough. I was constantly on guard, trying to please him, trying to get his love and approval. I had not yet realized I was in a no-win situation, which I was somehow determined to win.

HM had turned the sales territory around and was making great gains, when his old foe returned. I was waiting for him at the airport. The plane arrived, but he wasn't on it. I heard my name announced and went to a courtesy phone, almost in a panic from imagining something terrible had happened. I was so surprised to hear his voice that at first, I did not notice he was slurring his words — until I heard glass tinkling. As he explained why he had missed the plane, I realized the sound of tinkling glass was coming from the drink he was stirring in a bar.

From then on, our life was like a tragedy playing itself out. Late in the evening, I would call him at his hotel on the road and the clerk would tell me, "He hasn't come back as yet, Ma'am." My fear and tension mounted. Was he cheating on me? Was he laying, injured, in a ditch on the side of a road? I lived in constant anxiety. Often, my calls would go unanswered until three or four in the morning, when he would say he had been with his salesman. He drank more and more heavily, until he finally was unable to perform his job as sales manager. What had once been a promising career, filled with awards for superior achievement, was now crashing to an end.

In late August, he was drinking so much he could no longer drive, I drove our pickup camper from Detroit to St. Louis to bring him home. When I arrived, he was passed out on the floor. I asked the man who lived next door to help me put him in the camper, then I drove all the way back home.

I think he promised never to drink again. It happened so many times, I lost count. The next few months were a constant search-and-rescue mission. I would come home from work and HM would be gone. If he wasn't home by 10:00 p.m., I'd comb the area bars until I located him. Then I would plead with him to come home. (I did not know at the time that I was following a family tradition. My mother had done the same thing with her father when she was a child.) Several times, I took him to area hospitals for detoxification. And I fell apart a little bit more, with each occurrence. Once, a detox center orderly told him, "Why don't you just put a .45 to your head and do us all a favor?" At the time, I was shocked and outraged, but it was true. HM was killing himself little by little, and dragging us all through the painful process.

I began to attend open Alcoholics Anonymous meetings and joined a therapy group for women living with alcoholics. A few weeks before Thanksgiving, I sat in the back row at an open AA meeting, sobbing because of the pathetic situation facing me. At the end of the meeting, a kindly older gentleman approached and handed me a card. "Call that number and you'll feel better," he said. *Dial a Meditation* was the title on the card with a name — Jack Boland, Minister, Unity of the Infinite Presence — and a phone number. Every day, at work, I called the number and listened to the soothing voice.

The week before Christmas, HM was in a detox facility, again. When I visited him on Christmas Eve, he was unshaven and unkempt. He was so drugged that conversation was impossible. After our visit, I went to The Infinite Presence Unity church for the first time. As I sat in the last pew, choking back tears through the entire service, I couldn't get H.M's appearance out of my mind. The man who had once looked like my prince now looked like a derelict, a lost soul from skid row.

It was February; things continued as before. Each time I thought I couldn't take it anymore, I called the Dial-a-Meditation number and listened and cried. In therapy, I was learning about the rescuer/victim/persecutor triangle. And HM was drinking.

I was at my desk at work when my phone rang. "I just took an overdose of Valium and slashed my wrists. I want to die." HM's voice trailed off. I did not ask any questions — I knew all too well what he said was true. I called 911, then ran into my boss's office and explained the emergency.

As I raced to our home, almost certain that my husband was already dead, a new attitude came over me, amidst the fear and anxiety. I had heard of people reaching bottom, and I suddenly realized this was mine. I made a vow to myself that day: "If he lives, I am going to get healthy. If he dies, I am going to get healthy. This is it. I can't go on living this way."

The trip to the hospital in the ambulance only hardened my resolve. The emergency medical technicians explained that the slashes, although deep, weren't serious enough to cause death. The overdose would soon be remedied by a stomach pump. It was a cry for help, but I had finally reached the realization that it was a cry I could not answer. I could not solve HM's problems. I could only take hold of my own life, finally, and make the best of it.

The perspective of awakening has taught me what a blessing my relationship with HM really was. Without it, I would never have sought help. It was only because of this painful marriage that I woke up. I had to be brought to my knees.

Out of the Depths

After HM's physical recovery, we found a therapist who practiced Rational Emotive Therapy. Ned Papania set the stage by saying, "I'm not here to save this relationship. I'm here to help you both get healthy. And if that means the marriage stays, fine. If that means the marriage goes, fine." I did not know it at the time, but Ned Papania was one of those angels life sends you when you really mean business and want to change.

One day, Ned asked me why I had married an alcoholic, to which I proudly replied, "He doesn't beat me." Looking back, I realize that my main focus had been not to repeat the mistake my mother had made. HM did not beat me, therefore I had succeeded in my goal.

After two joint visits, Ned suggested we see him separately. Soon I was being encouraged to think for myself, to act for myself, and to let HM get his life together without my assistance. One day Ned said, "You are a very bright lady. But I think you turn your brain off when you go home from work." This led to a discussion of my childhood, and he explained that I wasn't using my brain at home because I had been taught to shut it off. I had learned this lesson well, and used it every time I had to ignore the violence in my childhood, every time I had to stuff my feelings, every time I had to pretend everything was okay when it wasn't, every time someone said, "I love you," and then abused me. My home life as a child had not been reasonable, but I knew from experience that questioning the things that did not make sense would only get me into trouble. Since our most basic instinct is survival, I had to shut down my reasoning power. Turning off my brain at home had kept me alive, and it had kept me sane. But I was not a child any more, and it was time to move on.

Ned was very perceptive, and very good at shaking me out of my complacency. "If a man who really loved you kissed you on the cheek, you would hit him," he said one day. "You don't know what true love is. And if you divorce HM without learning the lessons you need to learn, I guarantee your next husband will make this one look like a prince." That statement delivered more impact than anything I had heard, to date. When I asked Ned what I should do, he answered, "Get healthy within yourself. Make peace with your past, so when you and HM do part, you can look at each other, shake hands, and sincerely wish each other well."

I decided to do just that. But changing directions in life always brings new obstacles. The ones I faced now were the tasks of letting go of the past, forgiving those who had harmed me, and changing how I felt about myself — and what I believed I deserved. This would take a massive amount of effort, so I used every technique I could find, including affirmations, subconscious reprogramming, and meditation. I went to every seminar offered, and read every book I could get my hands on.

The most difficult part of my experience in therapy was making friends with my past. I had to look at my legacy and what I had done with it to date. The difficulty came when I decided everyone else in my family should also be involved. In fact, now that I understood the reasons for the turmoil I had experienced in my life, I thought I could help my family change, too.

The Legacy

The truth is, I was raised in a home very much like the homes of most children, both in the past and today: a home filled with love, confusion and despair.

My father drank to silence the demons within himself, and he lashed out at his wife and children when life got tough. My mother withstood the abuse because of her own low self esteem. She saw no other way to survive. My parents had each been raised in essentially the same way, and they knew nothing else. They taught me by example, to love others but to hate myself, just as they had been taught. How could they teach me differently?

When my dad was five years old, his father died. He was sent to live in an orphanage, despite the fact he had other brothers and sisters still living with his mother. His childhood was filled with the cruelty of considerable physical and psychological abuse, delivered by the very people he loved and needed the most. When he was 16, he was allowed to leave the orphanage, only to take a job in the tin mill. It was difficult for him to stay awake after working all night at the mill, so he was forced to leave high school in eleventh grade.

As an adult, my father believed his main duty to his children and to his wife was going to work every day. In 39 years at the mills, he only missed two days of work, so he saw himself as both a dependable and good provider.

Sometimes I wonder if my father stopped growing, psychologically and socially, during his early years in the orphanage. His behavior, when I was growing up, frequently mirrored the tantrums of a six or seven-year old boy. Unfortunately for all of us, when a 30-year-old man throws a tantrum, it has a much more profound effect on those around him than when he was six or seven. His uncontrolled anger sent several Sunday dinners crashing to the floor — tablecloth, silverware, dishes, food, and all.

My early childhood relationship with my father is best characterized by the fact that he called me Princess until I was seven years old. I loved him and he loved me. He was tall, with blonde hair and blue eyes, just like mine. We had happy times together when he took me fishing and allowed me to collect wild flowers, and when he took me with him to the tavern and set me up on the bar where his friends would buy me pop.

Then, somehow, as if by magic, one night — overnight — I became "bitch." I did not know what the name meant, but I could tell by his tone and the look on his face that it was not a happy name like Princess. No one ever explained what had happened, why I had lost the love of my dad. But I remember quite clearly the shock, the extreme disbelief, the overwhelming heartache, and the questions that ran through my mind. What had I done, or not done, to deserve his hate? What could I do to get his love back? It never entered my mind, as a child, that perhaps it was my father's problem — that perhaps some other, outer, circumstance had caused the change in his behavior — or that he might be mentally ill, or at least suffering from an addiction. How could a seven-year old understand such things? How could I have seen the thread that ran through my family — the thread of addiction and abuse?

Like my father, my mother had grown up in difficult circumstances. She had been forced to end her education in the eighth grade, to work in New York as a domestic. The money she earned helped support the remainder of the ten children at her parents' home. After her mother found her a better-paying job in a tin mill, she was allowed to return. She continued to work in the tin mill even after marrying my father, until their first child was born. After I came along, she helped make ends meet by working as a cleaning lady.

I remember the violence she experienced with my Dad, and how afraid I was. Maybe my mother's psychological growth was also arrested by the traumatic events in her life. What else would make a full-grown woman so afraid to take a stand? Why else would she be so fearful of the consequences of protecting herself and her children? I remember pleading with her, when I was twelve years old, to leave my father and all the abuse. But she was afraid. "How would I support all of you? she asked me. Even from a child's point of view, she appeared helpless and hopeless to me.

Imagine the despair I felt, as I learned from my mother how to be a woman in our world. Mother never had anything nice to say about being a girl. "In this man's world," as she called it. She told me women were treated as second-class citizens, who must tolerate plenty of pain and heartache from men. There was no beauty, femininity, or sweetness in the role of womanhood, as far as mother was concerned. There was only pain, drudgery, and the requirement to relinquish oneself sexually. Her life seemed to be living proof that these things were true. She shoveled coal for the furnace, stayed up ironing till 3:00 a.m., and waited on my father hand-and-foot. Often, I thought to myself, "Either I am crazy or my family is crazy. But I don't think this is the way it is supposed to be."

Our relationship was confusing to me. Mother had a policy of punishing first, then asking questions. When she found out she had acted in error, she would come to the sofa-bed I slept on at night, and ask me to forgive her. Even at the time, I did not understand why she would not just ask me about the situation first. One thing I am grateful for, is that she sincerely wanted me to have a better life than she had. Often, she told me, "Get an education, buy a car, see the world, and then think about marriage." This was not just a wistful wish, either. She made it quite clear that she expected me to do my very best in both school and extracurricular activities.

Looking back now, it is easy to see why my father and mother behaved as they did. Physical and emotional abuse were ingrained in their experience. I often say, "German shepherds learn to be German

Shepherds from German Shepherds." And, at age seven, I was a puppy in training.

Putting the Past Behind

Ned Papania helped me to see the legacy I had been handed — a legacy of problems, reaching far back, generation after generation. It seemed only natural to point fingers and lay blame, but Ned was also very clear that it was up to me to change. I could not continue blaming my parents or my past for my current conditions, because only I had made the choices and continued the behavior that kept me miserably married to HM.

Sifting through my family history, Ned helped me uncover the golden nuggets of blessings I had been too closely involved to see for myself. What my parents had actually wanted to teach me, by their example, was to work hard and unflinchingly, to be honest in my business and financial dealings, to go to church, and to be kind to those in need. My mother, in particular, taught me to apologize when you are wrong and ask to be forgiven. Ned also showed me what my parents *had not intended to teach me, also by their example:* never to trust my own feelings or to be honest about how I felt, that love and abuse go hand in hand, that I must never stand up for myself or question those who harm me, that I was worth less than other children, that life and especially marriage was full of pain and suffering, and that God was always watching and waiting to punish me. Of course, I learned far more from what I saw and experienced than from all the lectures I had ever heard.

It was also Ned who first taught me how to meditate. He called it self-hypnosis, and suggested books for me to read, then had me practice. One day, while I was waiting for my appointment in the lobby, I remembered an experience I had had several years earlier while on vacation in San Francisco.

I had been on a date until the wee hours of the morning, with a cable car driver I had met while sightseeing at Fisherman's Wharf. The evening had been a disappointment. Instead of touring exciting San Francisco night spots, I sat next to him at the bar while he conversed with his friends. After we had closed his favorite tavern he asked if I would give him a ride home. I was upset with his lack of communication with me but thought driving him home my duty. As we drove along the waterfront he asked if I would like to stop and walk along the beach. As we approached the water's edge, I was suddenly engulfed by overwhelmingly terrifying sensations. Although no one was touching me, I felt as if I was suffocating and being strangled. It was as if I was in the presence of Evil, itself.

I heard someone yell, telling me to get back to the car, fast. I ran at top speed, and so did my bewildered date. He jumped into the car's passenger seat just as I pulled away. I heard someone, again, yelling instructions to drive and not to look at "him." It was then I realized the voice was in my own head, and the "him" was my date.

Despite his constant efforts to have me pull over, explain my sudden odd behavior, or at least slow down, I managed to continue driving. Staring straight ahead, I called out for directions. Once at his home,

I stopped the car in the middle of the boulevard. Again, I avoided looking at him, even as he attempted to cajole me into coming up to his apartment, "to meet my mother." Finally, he go out of the car, and I sped away as if my life depended upon it. After a few blocks, the suffocating, evil, feelings began to leave me, and I drove back to our hotel.

As I remembered the incident, all the horror of the evil feelings returned. When I shared my memory with Ned, he said, "Karen, that is the difference between a live lady and a dead one. We all have an intuition that tries to warn us of dangers. But we don't always follow its guidance." From that day, Ned began teaching me to tune in to the voice of conscience within, to listen, and to act on what my heart felt was true. He began teaching me to trust myself.

My counseling sessions with Ned lasted two years. He found HM a job with another of his clients who owned a factory. HM stopped drinking, but our relationship never healed. After completing therapy, we began to study metaphysics but even our common beliefs did not help. In fact, we always had to buy two copies of each book, because we were unable to share with one another. We were like two ships passing in the night, like roommates who shared a bed, but very little else. It was during this time frame that I made my trip to Hawaii and was introduced to the idea of perfect partners.

A Fresh Start

I wish I could say that our exciting encounter after my Hawaii trip had renewed whatever spark remained in our marriage. At first, in my new flurry of optimism, I tried to remake HM into the perfect partner for me. I did not think it would be very difficult; not much needed changing. He was the right shape, the right religion. He had the right hair color and eye color. He had the right education. He had everything I wanted. We even danced well together. We looked good together. Everybody who saw us said we *looked like* the perfect couple. There was only one problem: he did not like me.

We were on our way to a boat show when I finally woke up. I had recently changed the shade of makeup I was wearing, and HM had not said a word about it, so I asked if he liked the change. He glanced at me quickly and said, "I've decided I like women who don't wear makeup and are more natural looking. And I definitely prefer darker hair."

I was incredulous. I had changed everything for him, and now he preferred women who looked exactly the way I had looked naturally, before??? Like a splash of cold water, the awareness hit me. I was still a seven-year old girl trying to get Daddy to love me. A circuit breaker switched off, inside me, that day. I finally saw the reality: there was no way for me to win HM's love.

Abandoning any further attempt to remake HM into my perfect partner, I turned my energy toward spiritual growth so I would not have time to pay attention to the pain in my heart. Ignoring my heart was not a conscious decision at the time. Nonetheless, we are talking Avoidance and Denial, big time.

It was only a few months since my awakening to the idea of perfect partners in Hawaii. I had been a student of *Unity* and *Science of Mind* for a total of six years. I had changed my life in many ways, but now it was painfully obvious that my marriage was still dead, a dud, a colossal failure. Both HM and I had come to realize that a bigger house, a newer Continental, and a larger cabin cruiser were not going to make us happier. I began to search in earnest for the *something else* that I knew was missing from my life.

One day after church, I confided to our Unity minister, Jack Boland, that I had still been unable to find that conscious contact with God, of which he spoke so often. When I asked what else I could do, he answered that I must learn to meditate. However, when I asked if he would be having a class on meditation that we could attend, he said, "No. You will have to go somewhere else for that." Funny, before this I had always looked at Jack as my mentor, as someone so far advanced of me. Now, he was just a teacher, a teacher who had no more to offer me.

My friend Jane thought I would find the path I was seeking at the Self-Realization Fellowship meetings which were held at the Detroit Institute of Arts. After several weeks of prodding, I finally agreed to go with her. As we entered the small auditorium, I was immediately repulsed by a heavy smell of incense. I was not very open-minded about anything I considered "weird stuff," and the music she called chanting, coupled with the incense, was far beyond what I called normal. I turned to leave, but Jane caught my arm. "Come on. Just stay through the service one time," she pleaded. But I was not listening; I just wanted to leave especially since I could see some East Indian guy's picture up on the altar, next to Jesus. My thoughts were racing: "Who could ever equate anyone with Christ? I am not into any Hindu-Shmindoo stuff. This is way too weird for me."

So I tugged against Jane's grasp, but she would not let go. Being seven inches taller and a proportional weight greater than I, she won the tugging contest and nearly wrestled me into a seat. But I got even; with my fingers plugging my ears, I refused to listen to anything during the whole hour. When the service was over, I quickly bounded out the door. Jane, a true friend, caught up with me again as I passed a book table in the hallway. "Buy the book," she said.

"What book?" I asked. She pointed to an orange-colored book with that Indian guy's picture on the front. It was titled, *Autobiography of a Yogi*. "I cannot even stand to look at that man's face, and you seriously think I am going to buy his book?" I protested with ridicule.

"Buy the book."

I knew by then that we could spend the next several hours arguing, unless I spent $2.50 on the book. Besides, Jane had driven us to the Art Institute and I needed a ride home, so it only made sense for me to buy the book — fully intending to throw it into the trash later. For some reason, when I got home, I shoved it behind the books in one of our book cases, instead. Either way, I was sure I would never see it again.

A year later, HM and I went to Cancun for a vacation. We were still together, still searching for someone to teach us how to establish that conscious contact with God. One day, while we were sunning on the beach, HM said, "Listen to this," and read aloud to me. I sat straight up and said, "Sounds like the technique we have been looking for. Where did you find the book?" Flipping it around so I could see the title, he said, "I found it stuffed behind all the other books in the living room book case." There it was, *The Autobiography of a Yogi* — the book I had wanted to trash.

Homeward Bound at Last

We spent more time reading the book than we did sightseeing. We were both engrossed in the ideals and principles expounded. After our vacation, I was sent to Los Angeles on business. I took the opportunity to look up a few of the philosophies I had been researching. One seemed too much like a Hollywood stage performance for me. The other had rules and regulations that seemed to depend upon the mood of the founding teacher. Then I went to Mt. Washington, to the Self-Realization Fellowship headquarters. The grounds were peaceful, the staff was very kind and obliging, but, still I did not feel at home with "that Indian guy," whom I now knew to be named Paramahansa Yogananda.

When I returned to Detroit, Jane was eager to hear about my visit. When I told her how I felt about Yogananda, she suggested I travel to northern Michigan to meet his oldest living disciple, J. Oliver Black. He was also known as Yogacharya Oliver, since *Yogacharya* is a title which means *teacher of yoga,* or *teacher of union with God.* Jane explained that Mr. Black had been a wealthy businessman, supplying parts to the auto industry in Detroit, before he met Yogananda. She thought we might hit it off, since we had similar backgrounds in business.

HM agreed to go with me to meet J. Oliver Black on Memorial Day weekend. When we arrived they were having a picnic at the retreat, which was called Song of the Morning Ranch, a Yoga Retreat of Excellence. We asked where Mr. Black might be found, and a staff member pointed to an elderly gentleman sitting at a picnic table. To be honest, I had expected a man in a turban and robes. Instead, Mr. Black looked like a normal, retired American businessman, wearing casual slacks, an off-white summer shirt that was open at the collar, and a tan hat to shade him from the sun. I sat beside him, on his right side, introduced myself and asked about the techniques I had read about in *Autobiography of a Yogi.*

Mr. Black's eyes studied my face before he said, "Your search is over. You are home at last." In that instant, I knew it was true. Here, at last, was the man who would lead me to God, Yogacharya Oliver. I later learned he was regarded as one of the great American Yogis of our time.

HM and I had finally found the spiritual teacher we had been seeking. We traveled to the Ranch every month and began studying the Self- Realization Fellowship lessons. Although HM and I were still unhappily married, it was much more tolerable now that we were focused on our individual spiritual growth. HM had not returned to drinking, and I was happier in my career than I had ever been.

Surprise, surprise

I had become a management trainer, traveling to various cities to present workshops and provide assistance to managers who were in the process of accomplishing personal and corporate goals. I loved my work, and would happily have worked twenty hours a day.

One day I was called into my manager's office for my yearly performance review. I had anticipated this occasion with joy as I knew I was considered one of the top trainers in the department and was excited about receiving an "outstanding" evaluation. As I examined the paperwork I became speechless. My eyes scanned back and forth between my name and the "satisfactory plus" evaluation score. I thought maybe there had been a mistake and I had been handed someone else's review.

After a few minutes of silence my manager, Tim C, asked, "Are you wondering where your 'outstanding' is?"

"Yes," I replied, bewilderingly.

"Well," he began to explain, "When you learn how to smooth the feathers in the right direction, when you learn to appease your peers and stop having to be so different, then you will get the outstanding you deserve."

I still didn't understand what was happening to me, how could I be receiving a "C" equivalent because of my peers when I definitely deserved an A+?

Noting my confusion Tim went on to explain more detail. "You are not very politically astute. You don't go drinking with the other trainers. You jog at lunch time instead of schmoozing with the group. You have to have special vegetarian meals provided at training sessions. And a lot of your peers just don't like you." He finished.

Now I was not only confused but also angry. The majority of my job as a management trainer had been to teach Participative Management. Some of the tenets of that style of management included management and staff working together towards goals, open communication and not allowing personality to affect job performance ratings. And here I was being downgraded because some of my peers did not like me! Because I had survived a heart attack and was improving my health with diet and exercise.

Yikes! There was nowhere mentioned that the other top trainers and I got along great. And, it was only the mediocre, low performers who complained about me. Why? Because I had come from Engineering and had not worked up the Personnel ladder. Plus, I was given some of the top assignments because I never treated employees differently regardless of their rank, foreman on the line or vice-president.

So, unexpectedly, through a set of painful circumstances, I chose to quit my most beloved, high-flying position. How could I teach participative management when I was not experiencing it in my own life?

HM was shocked by my announcement, which meant a significant lifestyle change for him, as well as for me. We had to give up the luxurious executive lease car, as well as the truck the company had provided for our use. How could we continue to afford the 36-foot Egg Harbor cabin cruiser on Lake St. Clair and our lovely Tudor style home in Rosedale Park?

Life had even more challenges in store for me, I soon discovered. Only nine days later, my father had a heart attack. Frantically packing a few things, I pleaded with HM to accompany me. In our ten years of marriage, he had only visited my folks twice. They were not "his kind of people." This time, he agreed. As we walked out the door, however, another call came in. I was too late. My father had died.

Our trip to Pennsylvania was accented by a unique sadness for me. Over the last few years, my relationship with my father had changed, once again. He had been open to my ideas about meditation and higher consciousness. He had listened to my frank assessment of his treatment of my mother and us children when we were young. He had been genuinely interested in improving as a person. Once, when we were alone, he had said, "You are the only one of my children that truly loves me."

Surprised, I asked, "Why do you say that Dad?"

"Because you are the only one that is honest with me."

At the funeral, my tears were not really for my dad. I cried because I had missed the chance to say goodbye to my dear friend, for that is how I had come to view him as an older friend, who was trying to learn and grow, just like me.

Back in Detroit, unable to submerge myself in work, I was also forced to face the reality at home. The buffer zone of activity and financial security had been removed from between us, and it did not take long before HM and I were discussing divorce. One evening, I decided I could not continue to live this way with HM for one more moment. Something had to change, and I knew it. I sat down in my meditation chair at 11:00 p.m. and vowed not to move until I received guidance about what to do. I was adamant, not one more day would be lived in this old way.

Over and over, I asked for an answer, to be shown what I was doing wrong, or what direction to take. Finally, at 3:00 a.m. I heard a bold voice, "Your life won't change until you change." In my mind's eye, I saw myself in Manhattan, attending an intensive workshop that I had been considering. A peace came over me, as if someone had wrapped me in a warm, loving, liquid blanket, and I knew this was the answer I had sought.

The Life Spring Beginner's Workshop was about taking personal responsibility for one's life. The work I had done with Ned Papania, so many years ago, had started me on this same path. Now I was ready to pick up where I had left off, and continue. I had to learn how I had created things, and how I had been the cause of everything in my life. I also had to confront the knowledge that living a lie only hurts everyone involved. That saying "I love you" just because it is expected in a relationship does not help to make it true. That every day I stayed in the marriage was as if I were renewing my wedding vows, saying and meaning "with this ring I thee wed."

I came home from that workshop knowing changes would be made in my life. In January, HM and I agreed to meet with Yogacharya to discuss our marital plight. I was surprised when Yogacharya recommended moving away from the city rather than getting a divorce. I could not understand how moving away from the city could improve such a pathetic relationship.

Now, I see that it was the wisest move. Now I realize that if I had divorced HM at that time, I would only have gone on to marry husband #3 at some point in the future, just as Ned Papania had warned me. And, just as he had warned me, husband #3 would have been someone who made HM look like a prince. Why? Because I did not know how to pick'em. And because the Universe has to "up the ante" until we get our lessons.

So HM and I moved 250 miles north of Detroit, where we could be closer to our meditation group. The move also allowed us to spend more time with Yogacharya, to whom I had written many times over the last few years, pouring out my heart to him about my desire for a perfect match. He had, in turn, been very open about his experience with his wife of 54 years, whom he described as his perfect spiritual partner, PSP. He told us that one sign of being with the right mate is always remaining sweethearts, no matter what storms come into your life.

Well, we were having storms. Without my high-paying position, life got pretty tough, and HM started drinking again. This time, I could neither ignore it nor bury myself in work, although I certainly tried. No, this time I had the unconditional love and relentless assistance of my spiritual teacher to guide me. When HM refused to come to evening meditation, Yogacharya would ask me, "Does he stay out all night? Does he come home drunk?" I was mortified. I could not understand why he would ask such embarrassing questions in front of a group. I thought he was mocking me and my situation. Sometimes, he would even ask, "Where's that man you call your husband?" But I still did not understand.

Even my mother tried to wake me up during a visit that Fall. With all the therapy and changes I had undergone over the years, my mother had also changed. Now, instead of paying lip-service to biblical phrases, she wanted to know why I was putting up with HM's irresponsibility. She wanted to know why I was the only one in the family who was working.

At Christmas, we returned to Detroit to be with HM's family. I called out, "Merry Christmas," to everyone as we entered his stepmother's home. The women were talking in the kitchen and barely skipped a syllable to wish us a happy holiday. The men, not even answering, remained glued to the tube in the living room, watching football. Suddenly, I felt alone, as if I were in a strange place where no one knew my name or cared about me. I decided to go to an upstairs bedroom and meditate, to calm my emotions. Ascending the stairs, I looked back at the male bodies strewn about the living room floor, and I murmured, "I am never going to spend another holiday this way. This isn't my family."

Still, I knew any decision to end my marriage would only come after I could clearly see that it was the best choice for me, so I made an appointment to speak privately to Yogacharya. We discussed my relationship with HM, how we had met and come to be married. Then I admitted that I had dated a very sweet man before I met HM.

Jack and I had both belonged to the Corvette Club of Michigan. We had a wonderful friendship, thoroughly enjoying each other's company and foiling each other with innocent banter until we rolled on the floor with laughter. One day on a picnic, he asked if we could go steady. I was shocked. I could see him as a dear friend, but I could not consider a serious relationship with a man who was so different from me. I pointed out that he was Catholic, while I was Lutheran. I was attending school to earn my degree, and he was just a repair technician. I was athletic; he had pins in his ankle and could not run to save his life. I loved to dance; he had two left feet. I made more money than he did. He wanted to do things for me, while I was busy being liberated. I had totally ignored the fact that we loved each other very dearly.

Yogacharya said, "You would have been much better off with a sincere friend," and I knew he was right. And then ventured to ask the question that was really at the heart of my concern. "I know it is my decision to make, but there is one thing you can clear up for me. Will it hurt my spiritual progress if I get a divorce?"

Yogacharya shrugged his shoulders, smiled, and asked, "Is this marriage helping your spiritual progress?"

"No," I answered, adamantly.

With an innocent look, he continued, "It is your decision to make, but I say that it is better to part, if you cannot live in harmony."

I felt as if a heavy load had been lifted from me that day, not because of Yogacharya's comment about parting, but because my spiritual growth would not be harmed. Self-realization had become the most important thing in my life, and I had been haunted by childhood religious beliefs that I was damned to hell for getting a divorce. That fear crumbled quickly, but Ned's prediction that I could attract someone who made HM look like a prince, if I did not get all my lessons loomed in the back of my mind. There was no way I wanted an even more miserable life!

That night as I prayed and meditated, asking to be shown the truth about the situation, the thought came, "The confusion comes from not following your heart, from wishing that things are different than they are, from not accepting the reality of things as they are." I had still been hoping, deep in my heart, that if I could just focus on the good in our relationship, and on the good that was in HM, then everything would straighten out. I had still been hoping he would finally see that I was a wonderful person, and would accept and love me.

The next day when I awoke, HM was in a nasty mood, quizzing me about our finances. He wanted to discuss a budget. I felt uncomfortable, anxious in the pit of my stomach, but I really did not know why. I just kept thinking that life was not supposed to be this ugly, this difficult. But whenever I contemplated divorce, there was some invisible thing holding me back, something I seemed to be confused about. I knew the relationship was wrong, but I could not seem to let it go. I was like an abused child who wants to go back to the parent that beats it, looking for the love and approval I had never gotten.

Was I afraid of making another mistake? After all, this would be divorce number two. Was I afraid that HM really was the right man and I would be losing him forever? Was I afraid that I really did not deserve true love?

I kept expecting the relationship to change, waiting for HM to turn into my prince and for us to live happily ever after. What was I doing wrong?

The next day, as I contemplated the situation, a question came to my mind: "If you were driving down a road and made a wrong turn, would driving thirteen more miles on that wrong road make it right?"

"What a silly question," I thought. Then I realized it was just the analogy my technical mind could understand. HM and I had been married thirteen years. It had been a mistake, and staying together another thirteen days, weeks, or years would not change the fact that we were mismatched.

What joy! There was my answer, just as simple as that. I had made a mistake, that's all. I did not have to pay for the mistake for the rest of my life. I did not have to keep sleeping in a bed that was no longer comfortable. In fact, if I stayed in the marriage now, I would be doing both of us a grave disservice. I was free at last.

A few months later, as I left the north woods to begin my new life, I was thinking about how wonderful it would be to have my perfect partner in my life. The thought came to me, "Three years," but I dismissed it. After all, I had already met the one I thought was destined for me. I had just become reacquainted with JB before leaving Michigan, and I certainly could not understand how it would take us three years to get together.

Seeing with the Heart

Now, the truth is: within three weeks of my divorce, I did actually meet my perfect partner. I just did not recognize him. After my divorce from HM, I moved to Milwaukee, where I had accepted a position as Department Manager in a small company. I had heard about a meditation group which met at the YMCA, so I attended one evening.

Instead of the peaceful calm I was accustomed to experiencing during meditation, this service seemed disjointed and the atmosphere was full of tension. I was grateful when it was finally over, and ready to run out the door when a man approached me. His name was Richard Bowen, and he said he recognized me from Song of the Morning Ranch. He also offered me his card and invited me to join a small group which meditated at his house. I was anxious to leave, and not at all interested in repeating the type of meditation experience I had just endured. When I assessed him as a possible perfect mate, all I could think of was: too tall, too thin, too young, wrong hair color, and he looks like a monk who has never done anything interesting in his entire life. I immediately threw away his card when I left the room.

Besides, I was sure JB had the potential to be the right mate for me. He was an airline pilot from Chicago, whom I had known for a few years. After my divorce, he had visited me in Michigan and had taken me to dinner several times. I was impressed with his attention, his social sophistication and his business savvy. Since I had moved to Milwaukee, he had been buying me dinner and flowers, and was showering me with attention, both over the phone and through surprise visits.

One evening, we met north of Chicago for dinner and an evening on the town. I planned to surprise him by driving up in my new car, a 944 Porsche. I eagerly awaited his reaction, since he was interested in sporty cars and drove a sleek Pontiac Firebird himself. I was especially proud of my new Porsche, and I hoped he would relish it and share in my happiness.

When JB pulled up, he was openly shocked and asked, "Where did you borrow the car? Is it a friend's?"

"No, Goose, it is mine," I replied.

"Follow me," he said, dismissing the subject and, with a wave of his arm, he drove off again. That was it. That was all.

I did follow him, to a restaurant a few blocks away, but he never even looked at my new car again. Not one more word was said about it. Although I tried to follow along with his line of conversation, my attention was caught up in wondering why he had ignored my happy event, puzzled at how someone who claimed to love fine sports cars could ignore a brand new 944 Porsche.

Later that evening, I realized our incompatibility reached a far deeper level than his mere inappropriate reaction to my new car. After dinner, we shared our very first kiss, and I knew in that moment that JB was not my perfect mate.

What was I doing wrong, I wondered. Maybe, I decided, over the seven years which had passed since the conference in Hawaii, I had forgotten some of the basic rules Robert Schied had laid out in his book. So I got another copy and reread it. Armed with new determination, a tremendous amount of experience, and refreshed knowledge, I struck out again to make my dream a reality.

I had only forgotten one important thing: *ripening is a process that can be aided or delayed, but cannot be forced.*

Although I was unaware of how much training I still required, the next few years were spent paring away at my prides and prejudices to prepare me for my perfect relationship. I wish I could say I did this willingly, but most of the time I was dragged, kicking and squealing, to my good. The first miracle I experienced during this time was the loss of my job as department manager. For the first time in my life, I stood in the unemployment line. I soon discarded the notion that only lazy, uneducated bums accept public assistance; it is just too bad the process has become such a humiliating experience. It also did not take me long to give up the idea that my job title, what I did for a living, and how much money I made were of central importance in life.

It was a "dark night of the soul" for me. I had always been able to live quite comfortably since I had begun to earn my own living. Now, I was unable to obtain even the most menial of jobs.

When I received no response to the resumes and cover letters I had sent all over the city, and all over the country, I began to search for any job: retail sales, telemarketing, secretarial and clerical positions, floor sweeper. "Over-qualified" was the term every potential employer used to deny me work. To me, that classification only meant more embarrassment in the unemployment line. Plus, the rent on my exclusive high-rise apartment overlooking Lake Michigan, the lease fee on my Porsche, and the grocery bill to put food on my table, were all quickly depleting my savings.

It was August when I attended the Satsanga (a gathering of truth) at Song of the Morning Yoga Retreat. I was completely humiliated by the state of my financial affairs. No, humiliation is too mild to describe what I felt. I was beyond discouraged, and approaching despair. The last thing in the world I wanted was to explain my failure to Yogacharya Oliver. This was the same man I had consulted during my disastrous marriage to HM, and I had experienced his sharply perceptive comments and no-nonsense wisdom in action before. I did not relish the prospect of being his target, in front of thirty or forty people at the Satsanga, so I cowered in the dimly-lit sideline of the gathering.

A Satsanga was one of the rare occasions when Yogacharya formally addressed a group and answered questions. Sitting off to the side, out of his line of sight, I had hoped to escape his notice. Of course, I didn't. When he looked directly at me, I expected to become the target for chastisement. Instead, when Yogacharya addressed me, he quietly said, "Don't try to make life happen. Just let life happen. If you try to make life happen you will upset the whole apple cart, and then you will never have what is highest and best for you."

It was as if he was reading my mind and offering me advice about my job search, as well as my search for the perfect partner. I instantly recognized the truth in his advice, for I had spent months trying to push open every door I saw. The more I had pushed, the more firmly they had remained closed.

My first awakening to the possibility of living by Grace, of trusting God to take care of me, came a moment later, when Yogacharya said, "The Infinite Consciousness has its messengers, and if you are willing to do its bidding, you will always be taken care of and no harm will ever come to you."

That single comment was so powerful, so boldly promising, so ripe with adventure and reward, that I needed to know more. "How do we do that?" I asked.

"You must always follow your intuition," he replied.

In that moment I felt more joy and more eager anticipation than ever before in my life. Oh, to be a messenger of God! To do God's bidding! What other work could be higher? What other work could be more fulfilling? To know God would always see to my needs and would protect me from all harm! It was, indeed, a gigantic promise. I knew then, that I would make this my goal: someday I would become a messenger of the Infinite Consciousness. Little did I realize the demanding course which lay ahead of me.

At the end of the session, Yogacharya said to me, with a smile, "Quit worrying. Get happy and stay out of debt. Quit trying to make life happen. Just follow your intuition and everything will be fine." He paused, then added, "It's not going to happen the way you think it should, so just relax."

And so it began; from that moment, I would attempt to do everything by intuition. After all don't we reach a distant goal by taking baby steps and practicing until we achieve the desired end?

Of course, as soon as the goal is set, the obstacles we must face line up squarely in front of us. My next set of life-lessons came from the men I met. I had never realized how many prejudices I harbored, nor the fact that I carried a subconscious checklist by which many men were excluded from the possibility of qualifying as my perfect mate.

The first man I met was eleven years younger than me. Even before we met, he was disqualified by his age. I remember telling the friend who offered to introduce us, "I don't want to date a baby." The next man was Jewish, and I came face-to-face with my preconception that my mate needed to be of the same religion. The process of awakening to my own prejudices continued as I met each man who challenged one more item on my "list." One was shorter than myself, one was bald, and one was homely.

I also became conscious of my tendency to "bend over backwards" to get approval or attention from certain men. I noticed that I even behaved out of character at times, so a particular man would like me. Chuck was a good example. We met on Labor Day weekend. As I walked along Lincoln Memorial Drive, at Milwaukee's lake front, he drove by in a Classic Corvette convertible. As you know, I love sports cars, so I gave him the high sign and shouted, "Great car!" A little voice in my head, which I had become accustomed to hearing, said, "He'll be back to give you a ride."

Sure enough, about five minutes later, the Corvette pulled up to the curb next to me. The driver yelled, "Want to go for a ride?"

"Wait a minute," I said, turning away from him. Just one month earlier, I had begun to make a conscious effort to follow my intuition in every aspect of my life. Now I needed a second to find out, through my intuition, if it would be safe for me to get into this particular car with this particular stranger. I could hear a group of boys in the car behind the Corvette say, "Go for it, lady." At the same moment I saw, in my mind's eye, an image of myself in the passenger seat, riding away in the car. I knew it would be safe.

"I am Karen W," I said.

"Hi, I am Chuck ." he replied.

After a short ride along Lake Michigan, he drove to a concession stand to get us a soda. As he spoke, I noticed Chuck was about 5' 8", a comfortable height next to my 5' 5". He had light brown hair, a stocky build, and was quite attractive. He seemed to be a nice guy and I knew intuitively that he had come into my life to help me learn a few lessons.

By the middle of our first date, a picnic on a bluff overlooking the lake, I had realized that Corvettes were about all Chuck and I had in common. He was obviously not the perfect spiritual partner I was searching for, but for some reason, I still wanted him to like me. Later, when we returned to my apartment, his first kiss was much too aggressive for me. I explained that I was not ready for anything more. He backed off, and left shortly thereafter.

After our second date, a very disappointing bike ride, then vegetarian lunch at my place, he became aggressive again. His kisses were so intimate, and he pressed his barrel chest into mine with such force that I thought my ribs may break. I decided to explain more clearly that I was not interested in casual sex; that I was, instead, looking for my perfect mate. Chuck replied with surprise, "It wouldn't be casual sex. We know each other." Finally, my persistence at resisting his physical advances paid off, and he relaxed. Just a few minutes later, he left.

While I knew he was not the perfect partner I was looking for, I continued to act as if I wanted the relationship to continue anyway. It was as though I wanted to convince myself that Chuck could be the right one, until I finally had an experience which taught me more in a few minutes than I had learned in a year of college.

Chuck had worked the midnight shift and called me at 7:00 a.m. with a request. He had hurt his back and wondered if I would help him by showing him some Hatha Yoga.

I said, "Let me check." Placing the receiver on the floor, I closed my eyes and asked the question, "If it is highest and best for me to see Chuck this morning, let me see him walking into the front door of my building."

Instead of seeing, with my mind's eye, him entering my apartment building, all I saw was fog. When I opened my eyes and glanced out the window of my 21st-floor apartment, I realized that fog had moved in over the lake. So I said inwardly, "I need more clarification."

This time, not only did I *not* see the picture I had requested of my inner vision, I also heard a resounding voice say, "No!"

I picked up the receiver and said to Chuck, "I'm not getting a clear answer."

That was an outright lie. I knew from experience that if I did not see what I had asked to see, the answer was *No*. In other words, it was not highest and best for me to see him that morning. And even after asking for more clarification and hearing a very clear, unmistakable "No!" I was pretending to be unsure.

"Well, what does it mean when you don't get a clear answer?" he asked.

"It normally means that I am not to do whatever I am contemplating," I said, apologetically.

"Well then, let's forget it," he said. "We can get together some other time. I'll call you when I'm better," he offered, as we ended the conversation.

As I placed the receiver in its cradle, a horrifying awareness came to me: I had almost acted against my own intuition just to please another person. I had almost acted against that inner voice I had been patiently, painstakingly re-establishing communication with, that part of me which always knows the truth. I had challenged and minimized the only true friend I had: the friend who had always been there to comfort me and to protect me from danger; the friend who had been with me from the very beginning; that Guardian Angel, Higher Self, who had saved me on the beach in San Francisco, who had spoken to me through my sister Claudia about marrying the college professor, and who had tried to safely guide me thousands of other times, large and small.

I fell to my knees, anguish overwhelming me, and thought, "Who knows what my intuition was protecting me from? Maybe Chuck would have been injured or killed in an automobile accident in the fog." How egotistical I had been. It now seemed ridiculous that I had been willing to ignore such a clear warning, just to impress Chuck by helping him ease his back pain.

I vowed never to allow my own desires to impress someone, or even to help someone interfere with the Divine Plan for my life. Then, an even more terrifying thought came to mind. By the time Chuck could have arrived at my apartment, the other tenants on my floor would have been gone to work. What if this was the day Chuck had decided to show me that it would not be casual sex?

He never did call again.

Trusting the Heart

It was not until about a month later, that I realized my Porsche was very similar to the men in my life: all looks, and no heart. Not only had I been praying to be released from the enormous financial burden of the Porsche, I disliked its poor handling characteristics and I was tired of keeping it in showroom condition. I had never owned a sports car I disliked more, and the financial burden became greater every day. More than half of my monthly unemployment check went to the lease payment, which still left me with insurance, parking, and gasoline expenses to worry about, not to mention food and rent. When the Porsche was finally repossessed, I felt a sweet sense of relief as the men from the finance company drove it away.

Later, as I walked in the park, I prayed quietly out loud. In just a few months, I had gone from very comfortable affluence to subsistence living. I had lost all of my financial foundation and was now reduced to relying on others for my daily needs. I had always been the one who had money to help others. Now I was the one in need, and it had not taken long to learn who my true friends were. With the Porsche gone, I would be without a car for the first time since I was 18 years old. Rude awakenings seemed to greet me everywhere I turned, and I began to wonder whether anything ever lasts.

In less than one year, I had gone through a divorce, left my beloved country home, sold my business, lost all my investments, then the job, now the car. It was obvious to me that money and material things, as well as fair-weather friends, could all be gone in a flash. So what could I rely upon? As I walked, I kept asking, "Is there anything of value that lives forever?"

And the answer came: "Only the love you give lasts forever."

With a tear in my eye, I thought, "Of course, love is the only thing we ever give that is important." Reflecting back over my life, I remembered the moments of love others had given to me. Though they had been only tiny, little feelings at the time, they were now so soothing, so healing, so good to remember.

As I continued to walk, I pondered the lesson the Porsche had given me. I had been seduced by the car's attractiveness at first, only to discover over time that it really did not perform well, required a great deal of my time and energy, and did not truly satisfy me. The men had been quite similar. They had often had no substance, much like HM who was good looking, but had never been my friend, nor even a real lover.

It was a painful awakening. "I keep getting caught up in the pretty packages," I thought, "but they are empty." It was even more painful to realize that, even after all the therapy, meditation, and searching, I still did not know how to find my perfect mate.

For the Christmas holidays, I went back to Song of the Morning Retreat Center in Michigan. My very dear friend and spiritual teacher, Yogacharya, greeted me warmly. The first evening, as I sat next to him at dinner he asked, "Well, have you found the right partner?"

"No, Sir, I haven't," was my reply.

Then he asked the group at the dinner table, "How do you know when you've met the right partner?" Several individuals offered ideas, ranging from good looks to common interests. He then asked me, "Why not pick the one that likes you?"

"They are usually creepy," I responded, not realizing what I had said.

Yogacharya leaned over and whispered to me, "You'll probably meet him within a week."

"That's not funny. You're joking with me," I retorted, aware of the jokes he liked to play. He turned away and continued to smile as we ate. But the seed had been planted, and I was almost unable to sit still during the remainder of the meal. "Am I really ready for this event?" I thought. "Oh my God am I ready? Will he like me?"

My entire visit to Song of the Morning was overshadowed by Yogacharya's comment. It is difficult to even characterize the state of mind I was in. As much as I loved visiting the ranch, I wanted to drive straight back to Milwaukee.

When I finally did return home, my eyes searched the face of each man who came within twenty yards of me. I was so excited, so overjoyed with the prospect of finding my perfect partner, no other thought could enter my awareness. Everywhere I went, every man I saw, inwardly I asked, "Is it you? Is it you?" I sang; I danced; I thoroughly celebrated the long-awaited event. At the same time, I was afraid. What if I was not really ready? What if he was ugly or, worse yet, what if he thought I was ugly? What if he thought I was weird? With my very unusual lifestyle, could there really be a man for me?

Well, as the week came to a close, so did my celebrating. I did not meet him. I did not meet anyone even remotely close. Had Yogacharya been playing another joke on me? Well, if he had, it had been a good one. I certainly had become totally preoccupied with the anticipated event. If I had met my perfect partner that week, I later realized, I would have overwhelmed him with my enthusiasm. He would probably have run the other way.

One day in January, walking my way back from the veterinarian's office with my dog, I saw a man jogging toward me. He wore a navy sweat suit with a matching stocking cap, and he smiled at me very graciously, nodding as we approached one another in passing. I thought I recognized him. When I turned to get another look, he was also looking back at me. Before I could say anything, he was off, running again.

Weeks went by, and I wondered whether I had missed recognizing my perfect partner. So much time had passed since Yogacharya's comment at Christmas. Then, in early March, an important insight came to me, as I walked along the lake.

154

"There is no such thing as a miss," I realized. "If you are following the inner guide, it is impossible to miss anything: a job, the right mate, whatever." The more I considered the idea, the more all-encompassing it became.

"No matter where I go or what I do, I can never miss what is rightfully mine," I concluded. It was a very comforting thought.

"My perfect partner and I *will* meet. It is inevitable," I said to myself. But it was taking so long, and I was frustrated. I wanted to know why. As was my habit, I asked inwardly.

The answer came swiftly. "You must love yourself first."

What a blow. Of course, it made sense, but I was so accustomed to thinking of myself as worthless. How could I love myself, with all my frailties? But if I don't love myself, how can I love him? No wonder we have not met. What an awesome thing to have to accomplish before I could meet my perfect partner! This could take years, I thought. Returning home, I dropped down onto the couch and began to cry under the tremendous weight of the task. "How can I love myself with all my frailties?" I asked, again and again.

"Love yourself by forgiving yourself," came the answer.

"How do I forgive myself?"

"By forgiving others," came the reply.

During the next few weeks I began the process of forgiveness. First, I wrote down the names of every person who had ever harmed me. Then, before I went to sleep, I went over the list. One by one, I called to mind the incident or the person, and imagined I was talking to them personally. I told them how much their actions had hurt me. After all the rehashing was complete, I ended by repeating the person's name, then saying, "I forgive you, I bless you, and I release you. You are free and I am free."

Every night I picked up where I had left off, and when I had finished the entire list I went back to the beginning. If I still felt any bitterness, pain, resentment, or dislike for the person when I read their name, I knew I was not yet healed. For those specific individuals, I repeated the whole process. I knew I would only be free, and the forgiveness complete, when all negative feelings had completely disappeared.

When I had finished forgiving others, I realized I needed to do the same for myself, so I made another list. I wrote down all the things I had ever done, said, or thought, which I felt I needed to forgive myself for. Each night, I picked up my list and called the incident up into my conscious memory. This time, instead of rehashing what had happened, I immediately affirmed to myself, "I forgive you, I bless you, and I release you. You are a wonderful person, Karen, and I love you just the way you are."

One day, as I was thinking how much better I felt about myself and the world in general, the thought came to me, "Love is of the heart, not the mind or body. When you love yourself, you don't have to have things like Porsches to make you feel good. And you would not go into needless debt, because that is an unloving thing to do, putting a strain on yourself."

There was my lesson: My feeling that I was always being punished, of never being OK no matter how hard I tried, of being unworthy — they all stemmed from a lack of self-love, which only I could remedy. Through the process of forgiveness, I was getting a pretty good head start.

I was beginning to feel very good about things, but I was still anxious to meet the mystery man in the navy jogging suit. I was so eager to meet my perfect mate, and this man's existence on the outskirts of my life was so intriguing, that I began to convince myself that he *must* be the one for me. For several weeks I noticed which apartment building he entered, which car he drove, the type of clothes he wore, and any other clues I could gather to give me an idea of what he was like. Could he be my perfect partner? Was it time for me to meet him, now that I had taken great strides toward self-love?

It was a Saturday, and I had taken the bus to Mayfair Mall for some window shopping. The central portion of the mall is glass, rising like a cathedral, five stories high. It was a very inspiring view. I was feeling light and happy, learning to follow my intuition. On the second level, I noticed some beautiful wedding rings in a jeweler's window. I was soon talking to one of the sales clerks as she showed me all the new designs. Unexpectedly, she handed me the most beautiful wedding ring I had ever seen — a quarter-carat marquise diamond set in a filigree design of butterflies and hearts with a matching wedding band. I knew at once that this was the ring for me. I asked how much the ring cost and what the difference would be if I had an amethyst instead of the diamond. What joy, what a sweet surprise. But why was I finding the wedding ring before I even met my perfect mate?

I was accustomed to walking at least 6 miles a day, and when I got back from the bus ride it felt like time to exercise. As I walked across the Brady Street bridge down to McKinley Marina I was pleasantly surprised to see my mystery man's car. What joy! As I eagerly began the route around the lagoon, I was stopped short by the sight of him with another woman. They were holding hands like lovers and walking along the lagoon near the cattails. "Oh my God," I thought. "I just found the perfect ring, and now he is with another woman."

I hoped against hope: Is this just a friend? His daughter? When I turned back to see them once more, they had put their arms around one another. There was my answer: he is not mine; he is someone else's. Although we had never really met, my fantasy had become so real in my mind, I was devastated, but I caught myself quickly and affirmed, "There must be someone better for me." Then I asked inwardly, "Is there a man for me, the perfect, tailor-made man?"

"Yes," was the answer.

I walked another two miles, then headed back to my apartment. My shoulders were tense, as they often were when there was something wrong. I had learned that body signals were part of intuition and tense shoulders indicated a problem. But I did not know what the problem was this time. I immediately sat in prayer and released and blessed this mystery man.

I guess I had not really released him, in my heart. A few minutes later, I saw him when I took my dog outside. The thought came that I should turn around, but I continued. Finally, he seemed ready to meet me, waiting there on the sidewalk as I approached. I had invested so much emotional energy in imagining this man was my perfect partner, I began blocking out any signals to the contrary, even the knowledge of his embracing another woman in the park.

The dream I had created began to unfold, as WR and I met that day. He started the conversation by saying that he had been noticing me, too; because I walked so often. He wondered if I had lower back pain, as he did. He explained how he used physical activity in an effort to relieve the problem. Still, he experienced pain regularly, and was hoping for new insights from a fellow sufferer. I, on the other hand, was sure this was just a ploy of the Divine, to bring us together.

Though I was elated to finally begin developing a relationship with the man I thought was my perfect partner, there were numerous signs to the contrary. From the very beginning, I was uncomfortable with little things, jokes I did not understand that seemed derogatory, and random comments. But I shrugged them off. I also shrugged off the tension in my neck and shoulders, but I consciously noted that his eyes seemed cold, or calculating, or distant.

Another Lesson

The next day was Thursday, April 7th. I was following my intuition as it led me to take the bus to a shopping mall and then to get groceries. I was also thinking how perfect and easy my life was and how I much preferred the spiritual life, with God guiding my every step. I was happy not to have to decide anything, except, of course, to ask for guidance and then to follow what was given. I prayed that I would always live my life this way, for I had never before had such a perfect life.

My apartment was perfect, situated on the south side of the 21st floor of the Prospect Tower. It had ceiling-high windows with views of Lake Michigan, the Art Museum, the lagoon at McKinley Marina, and spectacular unobstructed sunsets over Milwaukee's skyline. I had the Oriental furniture I had always loved, I had found work in my own field with a good income, "Divot" the perfect cat, "Christmas" the perfect dog, and now, I thought, my life with my perfect partner, WR, was about to begin.

As I knelt in prayer to give thanks for all the perfection in my life, it came to me, "You get what is perfect for you because you always ask for perfection. If you did not ask, it would not be given. You get whatever you ask for and are willing to accept."

Then I remembered Yogacharya's little saying, "Life is great if you don't weaken." I had asked him once what it meant. He had said, "As long as you follow your intuition, life is easy and wonderful. But if you give in to your ego, well, then life is a different story."

That very evening, as I demonstrated six Hatha Yoga postures that would help WR's back, the most upsetting aspects of his character were revealed to me. I admired his quick wit, but his bawdy sense of humor seemed inherently disrespectful of women. He also used raw, profane language that made me very uneasy, but the conflict between our religious outlooks seemed almost irreconcilable to me. When I had mentioned intuitive decision making and tried to give examples of how effective the method was, WR said he did not believe in those fads. "As long as you're not one of those Jesus freaks, or the kind of person that talks to God," he quipped.

His statement took my breath away. Was he joking? Did he really dislike people who had faith in a personal deity? So I asked, "Are you joking or are you telling me that you don't believe in God?"

"No, I'm not kidding. I don't believe in God, I am an agnostic," was his abrupt and no longer humorous reply. Then he continued soberly, "I think people who have to have a God are silly and childish and foolish."

Despite this clear indication that we were ill-matched, WR and I spent more and more time with one another over the next few months, but never on a real date. His parents were moving back to Hamburg to retire. WR was not sure what he would do, since they had all agreed to close the family business in Milwaukee. I offered to help him narrow down the field of possibilities. I researched investments, homes to buy, businesses here and abroad, career changes, even a move to New Zealand or Australia.

Sometimes he seemed genuinely thankful that I was helping him with things he just did not have time to do. Other times, he seemed irritated with my interference or would respond sarcastically to my ideas. We spoke on the phone daily, often for hours. Still, there was no change in the form of our relationship.

When I presented my intuition with the question, "If WR is my perfect partner, let me see his face," I saw only blackness. I shrugged it off and redoubled my efforts to get his attention. In fact, I spent most of my energy during this time arranging to be wherever I knew he would also be. I thought that somehow, I could finally make him see me in a romantic way, to show him how wonderful I was so he would fall madly in love with me. When I could not go places to bump into him, I left notes in his mailbox or I surprised him with cookies I had baked. He would smile, say thank you and close the door. Or, he poked fun at me, saying, "Don't tell me, you made too many cookies, again."

In one of our phone conversations, the subject of marriage came up. He indicated he was not interested in finding a wife, and she would have to be someone he really enjoyed looking at, if he was. I felt upset. When was he ever going to become interested in me?

Another Turn

It was January, and over a year had passed since I had been to Song of the Morning. As I sat at the dinner table next to Yogacharya, I mentioned my perplexing situation. "I have met a man, but our relationship doesn't seem to be going anywhere. I can't even say that we are true friends."

"Maybe that is the way it is supposed to be," he countered. That knowing look was on his face. Had I just spent eight months trying to *make* a relationship happen? Had I been mislead by my intuition?

After the weekend, as I drove back to Milwaukee, I kept asking to be shown the truth, and all I could think of was, "Even if WR *is* my perfect spiritual partner, I don't want him. He is just not sweet enough to me." In fact, I caught myself repeating that phrase, over and over, with more and more conviction. Why had I been so willing to go against what I felt was true in my heart? Why should I have to settle for a man who obviously was not interested in me? "No," I argued, "I am not going to do that. If God thinks that WR is the right man for me, then He is wrong."

By February, I had decided, no matter what, WR was not my perfect mate. He was not nice enough to me, our lives were headed in two different directions, and, most importantly, I did not feel good when I was with him. That was it! That was the answer! Why hadn't I seen it sooner? It was so simple.

"If you follow your feelings there are no questions."

I had known at the start, from all my misgivings. I had known by how he treated me, but I had still clung to the dream. I had wanted so much for the relationship to work. I had been in love with the dream that WR was my perfect mate, but I had never been in love with him. The truth was now clear: my intuition had never misled me, it had been constantly trying to guide me, through my feelings. It was I who had ignored the subtle warnings.

When at last I released the hope and dream I had created around WR, I was left with both a sense of relief and an old frustration. If WR was not my PSP, then who was? And when would I ever meet him? Was there truly someone for me, or was I just kidding myself? I began to doubt that there could be a man who suited me. My way of life was so different from all the men I had ever met. Maybe I was too weird for anyone to ever be compatible with me.

As soon as I caught myself thinking that way, I reversed it and affirmed, "There is a perfect partner for me, and he will like me as much as I like him." I could feel that I was back on track, but one thing bothered me. I still did not know how to attract only the right man. Yes, I now had learned to pay attention to my feelings, since they are messengers for my intuition. But I was afraid there was still a missing link. After all, I realized, I had tried to *make* it work with WR, not by changing myself, as I had done with HM, but I had still tried, nonetheless.

"Will I ever get it right?" I asked.

It is funny, that mathematics can be learned easily, even algebra and differential equations. But when the subject is relationships, sometimes it seems to take forever to learn a few simple lessons.

Over the next few weeks, I concentrated on learning what the missing ingredient was. I reread my journals and Emerson's essay, *Spiritual Law*. I meditated and walked along the lake, pondering the issue. Finally, it clicked. "To thine own self be true."

"I do not have to go anywhere special. I do not have to act a part. All I have to be is myself. Finding my perfect partner is natural." By trying to *make* things happen, I had gotten myself way off base. It was actually pure grace that I never dated WR.

I suddenly felt lighter, as if I had passed a very difficult exam with flying colors. Twirling around like a ballerina, with my cat nestled in my arms, I shouted, "Thank you. Thank you. Thank you," to the Universe for saving me from myself. I ran to the window that looked out over the lake and shouted, "WR, I bless you! I release you! I set you free!"

Then I began a new song, "I can hardly wait to see, what kind of man you have for me."

Each night, in bed, I imagined how it would feel to have him at my side, how it would feel to lay in his arms. My imagination was so strong that one night I actually felt as though someone was in my bed. I opened my eyes; no one was there. Perhaps it was a physical premonition?

Then one day as I walked, I realized how happy I was, even without my perfect partner. Life was good, when I followed my intuition. Everything fell into place when it was supposed to. If I found my perfect partner, would I have to give up my great life? I did not want to do that. But I did not want to give up my desire for a beautiful relationship, either. I began to battle doubts, then I realized that what I really needed to do was just surrender. I prayed with all my heart, "Heal me so I may attract the one that You have chosen for me. I want no other."

Never Judge a Book by its Cover

The next day was July 13th. Although I really did not want to, I followed my intuition and attended a

165

meditation group at the YMCA, which I had purposely avoided. It was the same group I had visited three years earlier, just after my arrival in Milwaukee. That experience had been unpleasant enough to keep me away forever, but my inner guide had insisted, so here I was.

The service was already underway when I arrived. Slowly opening the door to the chapel, I entered quietly and sat in the back of the room. The air was thick with the wonderful fragrance of incense. The altar was bright, with candles illuminating pictures of great saints. The atmosphere in the room was peaceful. This was in sharp contrast to the last time I had been here, when all I had sensed was restlessness and negativity. At the end of the service, a man with reddish-blonde hair approached me. I recognized him to be the same man I had met the last time I was there. Again, my mind immediately categorized him as too tall, too thin, wrong color hair, looks too young and inexperienced, like a monk who has never done anything interesting.

"Where have you been for the last three years?" he asked. I was amazed that he not only remembered me from my one previous visit, but that he also knew exactly how long I had been away. Although he seemed pleasant, his question carried a bit of sarcasm, so I replied with an equal edge, "My intuition never told me to come back, so I didn't."

He responded, more sharply this time, "Since when does God keep you from meditation?"

Feeling as though I had been stuck by a barb, I retorted, "I didn't say He did. He only kept me away from this group." Then I thought, "Who is this guy, anyway, asking me why I have not attended *his* favorite group meditation?"

Another member of the group overheard our conversation and offered an explanation. "She probably stayed away because she could feel the in-fighting that's been going on between the members these last few years." I smiled and nodded my head in agreement.

Several others in the group recognized me from Song of the Morning Retreat and invited me to accompany them to a nearby restaurant for coffee and dessert. It was just my luck that the tall, thin man with the sharp tongue sat right next to me. I discovered his name was Rich and that he had seen me several times at the retreat in Michigan, as well as walking my dog along Prospect Avenue. He had a contagious sense of humor, and I soon found myself laughing at his jokes. "I guess he's not a pious monk after all," I thought, "and maybe he's not as young as he looks, either." It was a hot summer evening, and I had noticed a few gray hairs peeking out at the open neckline of his shirt.

As usual, my intuition had been right. I welcomed the peaceful atmosphere of the meditation group, as well as the social contact with like-minded people. I began to attend regularly on Thursday evenings, and was soon participating in the group's social activities. The first was a meditation and picnic in Fond du Lac. Jill, another member of the group, called while I was preparing to leave.

"Would you like to ride with Rich and I up to the picnic?" she asked.

"Let me check inwardly. No, I'll drive by myself. Thanks anyway."

I arrived before Rich and Jill. During a tour of the property, the time to meditate came and went. I wondered about the delay.

"Weren't we supposed to begin meditation at 1:00 p.m.?" I asked Tom, the host.

"Yes, but the leader isn't here yet. I'd rather wait until he arrives."

"Who is going to lead today?"

"Rich Bowen from Milwaukee."

As we finished the tour, Rich and Jill arrived, over an hour late. "What happened?" Tom called out.

"There was a lot of construction and slow traffic," replied Rich.

"Gee, I didn't run into any traffic," I teased. "Did you follow your intuition?" Rich shook his head as he unloaded the car.

As we sat to meditate, Rich began to play his guitar, beautiful, soul, sweet music, enchanting, beckoning, and peaceful. A tear fell from my cheek. "When am I going to find my partner? Why can't he be a beautiful spiritual man?" I realized then, that I was attracted to Rich, but I brushed it off because I thought it was just the effect of his sweet music. His devotion for God was evident in the music he played, and the resonant chord it touched in me, made me ache for a soul-mate to share my path.

After meditation, we all went to Lake Winnebago for a potluck picnic. The food was excellent. Then we played volleyball, followed by a walk around a lagoon. Tom and I walked ahead. This was our first meeting, but I felt very comfortable with him. He was my height, with long brown hair, a square jutting chin, and merriment in his eyes. He spoke of his search for a mate and all the disappointments of meeting people in bars.

"I'm about as lucky in love as Richard is," he said.

"What do you mean? He's never been married has he?" I inquired.

Tom began to laugh, one of those belly laughs that will not let go. "Never married!? He's been married and divorced twice!" I was shocked. Rich did not look old enough to have been married twice.

The next Thursday meditation was a commemorative service. Each person laid a flower on the altar and offered a special silent prayer. As each person took his turn, the others sang softly in the background. The ceremony was very sweet and touching. I had my eyes closed most of the time, but for some reason I looked up just as Richard approached the altar. He looked very humble as he placed his flower and knelt in front of the altar. "What devotion he has. I can feel the sweetness in his heart," I thought. "It is odd that I can't feel that devotion from any of the others."

The next Sunday our group went to German Fest at the water front. Rich asked me to get soft drinks with him. He began talking about his trip to Europe.

"When did you go to Amsterdam and Greece?" I asked.

"Oh, that was about twenty years ago, on my honeymoon."

"Your honeymoon? I thought you just got married five years ago."

"That was my second marriage. It only lasted 14 months."

Not revealing the information I had received in my conversation with Tom, I remarked, "Wow, you are about as lucky in love as I am. I've been married twice myself."

"I knew your husband HM from Song of the Morning ranch. I did not know you had been married before that."

After making the rounds of all the exhibits, music shows, and ethnic foods, Jill asked if anyone wanted to attend a Beethoven concert with her that evening at the amphitheater. Both Rich and I raised our hands. There would only be the three of us. Later, Jill decided she did not feel well and went home, instead. Rich and I attended the concert, anyway, and had a marvelous time. Our conversation continued to be punctuated by good-natured banter. After the concert we walked through the park and stopped for frozen yogurt.

"At the ranch last summer, I met a woman named Joanie, who was one of the sweetest women I have ever met. Do you know her?" Rich asked.

After a great evening, for the first time without the rest of the group, he was talking about another woman. My ego was crushed. "No, I can't say I do."

As Rich continued to describe his meeting with Joanie, all I could think was, "He doesn't see me that way. Maybe I am too boisterous. Maybe I should act more demure." Then I became aware of my self-talk, and stopped it immediately. "No, I am not going to act a part. I am sweet in my own way, and the right man will see that and be attracted to me."

As he dropped me off under the canopy of my apartment building he said, "Maybe we will see each other again next Thursday, if the spirit moves you."

"That's a dig. Are we even now?" I replied.

"I guess so."

After he drove away, I considered how different he actually was from what I had judged based on his looks. He no longer seemed too tall, too young, or too thin. And he certainly did not look like a monk to me anymore.

I was still in the lobby when I heard a horn. It was Rich. He had forgotten to return the sweatshirt I had loaned him for the evening. As he drove away one more time, I thought, "I just want him to be who he is, and who he is not. And I want to be healed, so I can attract my perfect mate. I must be me, at all costs."

The next week found me tailgating before the Milwaukee Brewers game with Jill and Rich. He seemed to delight in jabbing me with somewhat caustic remarks about my previous marriage. "Don't you think you're getting a little personal?" I asked.

He changed the conversation to his writing business, explaining his desire to start his own company and break away from the large corporation he worked for.

"I need help promoting some workshops. Can you do brochures?" I asked.

"Sure, that is my forte, along with copy editing."

I was elated that we could barter services. I could see his sincerity and offered to help. I explained my background, that I had also started my own business after working for a corporation, and offered to share my ideas. He seemed genuinely interested and I felt pleased that he treated me with more consideration afterward.

The experiences of the last three years had taught me the importance of being myself, and I planned to cheer, hoot, and holler at this baseball game, as if I were alone. I was surprised that, inside the stadium, I met a whole new Richard. Sitting between Jill and me, he was clapping, yelling and cheering. The Brewers center fielder hit a home run, and before I could even jump out of my seat to scream, Rich was far ahead of me, yelling. When he slapped me on the back as if I were one of the guys, my thought was, "Well, he's not so bad after all."

During the seventh inning stretch, we went to get refreshments. As we chatted, I told him that I used to race cars for excitement. He said he had never really been very interested in cars and had experimented with hallucinogenic drugs, instead. I nearly fell on the floor. This guy looked like someone who had never done anything of interest in his life, let alone anything very demanding or courageous. Now he was telling me he had done things I would never even have dreamed of doing, like leading a strike and demonstration at his high school that had shut the school down. Hey, I was Miss "Play It By The Rules" in school.

"Boy, you've done things I would never dream of. I am amazed. You look like such a purist."

"You've only known me a few weeks. How can you make a judgment like that?" he asked.

As we continued to converse, I found out that both his marriages had been similar to mine. He ended the topic with, "I am really happy, being free as a lark and not having to check in with a wife."

Well, that was enough for me. He could not be my perfect partner if he did not even want to be married, but he certainly was helping me to learn never to judge a book by its cover. "I have been wrong about everything about him so far, and that lesson is prize enough for me," I thought.

A New Adventure Begins

It was Thursday, August 3rd. I was a consultant at a computer sales corporation. At the job site, I checked for messages and found that my trip to California, scheduled for August 15, had been cancelled. I was happy to give up a three week computer class in Los Angeles.

The first person I called was my friend, Joan. Then I made reservations for the weekend at Song of the Morning ranch. Finally, I called Rich to say I would be in Kenosha on business that afternoon. I wanted to pick up a book he had borrowed from a friend for me. It was good timing for him, and he suggested we also discuss the details of bartering our services.

It was an hour-long drive to Kenosha and when I arrived at his apartment, I looked like a wilted flower. The temperature was 90° and my car had no air conditioning. I had been in my business suit for almost ten hours, but it looked as if I had slept in it for three days.

"Can I use a washcloth and your bathroom?" I asked.

"Sure," he said, and disappeared into the bedroom quickly. When he returned, he had not only a washcloth, but also a pair of shorts and a tee shirt.

"I'm not staying that long," I protested.

"You will be more comfortable in these." He handed them to me and smiled.

When I got out of the bathroom, he had already made some limeade from his own recipe, and motioned for me to sit on the couch in the living room. I noticed that his apartment was very neat, with just enough furniture to make it comfortable. Potted plants covered a long table in front of the three windows in the living room. An archway separated it from the dining room where his computer was set up. The kitchen was closed off by a door.

We were together for nearly seven hours, talking about everything from business to past marriages and yoga. The time went by very quickly, and I felt very comfortable with him. I could see it would be easy for us to work together. We meditated for an hour and made a simple meal together, then continued our discussions. Again, I noted, he mentioned how happy he was to be single.

The next day at work, everyone seemed to be avoiding eye contact with me, but I brushed that awareness aside. The General Manager had left a message on my computer, asking me to stop by before I left for my half-day of vacation. I was leaving early to drive to the meditation ranch.

George was unusually business-like when I entered his office. He motioned for me to sit down and said, "I can't believe I have to do this," as he handed me a sealed envelope. I sat down and opened

174

it. A letter explained that my contract was being cancelled because the company was experiencing a serious downturn in sales. They were cutting back nationwide. Two checks were enclosed: my last paycheck and a severance check.

There was nothing more to say. I packed my personal belongings into a box, turned over my keys and security card pass, and walked to the parking lot. I was free.

It was 12:30 in the afternoon. I knew Rich was leaving the next day for a week-long convention in Los Angeles, so I decided to leave a message on his answering machine at home. Instead, he answered the phone.

I told him about my contract being cancelled. "I guess I will be able to help you with your business a lot more than I thought, at least until I find another consulting position." We finished our discussion and agreed to get together when he returned from California.

I arrived at the ranch late in the evening, and spent the next day blissfully walking along the shore of Lake Michigan. It was a beautiful, delightful summer day. I returned to the ranch in time for dinner. After meditation, I sat near Yogacharya and listened intently as questions were asked about marriage and how to get along. One man asked what he could do to help his marriage; he felt he had given all he could, but still they fought.

Yogacharya smiled and offered, "Remember, giving is the law of getting in everything. But you must give freely or it is not a gift." He continued, "Women are the easiest beings to get along with. I don't understand why men have trouble with them. All you have to do is truly love them and they will do anything for you. Isn't that simple enough?"

The crowd broke out in laughter at the difficult problems, made easy by his wisdom.

Later, I whispered to him, "I am looking for the guy that will like me just the way I am and that I can like in the same way."

"Good," he replied as he patted my hand.

After the trip to the Ranch, I went to Pennsylvania to see my family. The week went by quickly, visiting old friends and relatives. I was back in Milwaukee on the Saturday Rich was to return from California. I called to leave a message, on his machine, welcoming him home. Again, he answered the phone instead.

"I've been trying to reach you," he said.

"Why?"

"I wanted to know when we could get together and start working on my business."

"Well, I am sure you're tired from your trip, but when did you have in mind?"

"How about later on this evening?" he quickly replied.

"Are you sure you want to get together so soon?"

"Yes."

"Okay." I was surprised that he was so eager to start working with me. We agreed on a time and I hung up.

Rich lived in an upper flat with an outside doorway leading to a staircase, but he answered the door so quickly, it was almost as if he had been waiting at the bottom of the steps.

176

"Before we get started, Rich, there are two things I have to clear up with you. First of all, do you have any tortilla chips for the dip I brought? And secondly, if the Universe wants you out of your current position before the end of the year, will you put your ego aside and just surrender to that?"

He laughed, "Yes, I do have chips, and I have already decided I am ready for a big change. Whenever the move is right, I will make it. But I have something to ask of you, too. Before we get started, can we set the mood right by meditating briefly?"

"My thoughts exactly." I replied.

I was touched that he had set up a small altar and placed a picture of Yogacharya near it. "How very thoughtful of you, Richard."

We were together from 8:15 in the evening, until 3:45 a.m. There was so much to talk about. We discussed business possibilities that ranged all the way from running a health food store to bottling and distributing a salad dressing and a lemonade product that he was considering patenting. We finally settled upon freelance writing.

The next morning, my mind was full of ideas to help Rich begin pressing forward with his business. I called after noon to share them with him.

"I was just going to call you," Rich chuckled. "Would you like to go on a yogi picnic?"

"What is that?" I questioned.

"Well, we can invite Jill and Rose. Then you can pick them up and come down to Racine for a picnic."

"No, Rich. You can call Jill and Rose, but I am not bringing them anywhere."

"That's not a nice attitude." He replied.

"Well, I am trying to follow what feels best, and that is what feels best to me. Should I apologize for that?"

"No."

"Great. Then you do your thing with Jill and Rose and call me back." As I hung up the phone, I felt that old tension-in-the-neck feeling. "Isn't it interesting that whenever I tell someone something I don't think they want to hear, I get tension in the neck."

A few minutes later he called back. "Jill and Rose are both busy today. Want to go anyway, just the two of us?"

"Sounds great to me. What do you want me to bring?" I offered.

The park in Racine had secluded areas, but they all seemed filled with either children or bugs. The Frisbee flew, but it was not much fun between swatting mosquitoes. The avocado sandwiches were great, but the flies seemed to carry half of them away. We agreed to look for a better spot.

Racine Beach was almost deserted, quite a surprise for a Sunday afternoon. As we walked barefoot through the water, the gulls flying overhead, I thought how gentle Richard was, "He loves nature and silence. It is almost as if I am by myself. I like that." The afternoon flew by, blending into evening.

"I am getting pretty hungry, Karen. Would you be interested in a nut loaf that I could whip up real fast?" He suggested

The ingredients went together so easily. I chopped the onions and cut up bread crumbs, while Rich chopped the nuts and added the eggs and cheese. Neither of us said a word; we just worked together as if we were harmonizing in a duet we had sung many times.

When the loaf was in the oven, Rich prepared to meditate. Placing his blanket close to mine, he removed his shirt to counter the temperature of the room. As we sat next to each other, my eyes opened for a moment and I glanced at him. His face was so serene, almost angelic; it revealed no signs of age, only tranquility. He seemed regal. I had never actually noticed his face before. I had never realized how very handsome he was, until this moment. It was as if I was seeing him, for the very first time, as he really was, regal and serene. A warm energy surrounded my body, as if our auras were flowing together and meshing. "I can easily see us as lovers, laying in each other's arms," I thought, and a tear formed in my eye, for my blindness.

Dinner went as easily as the preparation, and I automatically began washing the dishes as Rich put the food away.

"Are you ready for some entertainment?" he called out from inside the refrigerator.

"What do you have in mind?" I asked.

After disappearing into his bedroom, he returned, guitar in hand, strumming and singing an old Beatles song. What delight! His eyes flashed as if he were on stage; I danced and clapped my hands to the music. Song after song: Bob Dylan, Jefferson Airplane, songs I had not heard in a long time. This man was definitely not a monk.

We spent hours talking again, until shortly after midnight, when I began feeling it was time to go.

"Would you like to come over tomorrow and start with some of our ideas while I am at work?" Rich asked, as I gathered my things to leave.

"You mean, would I like to come over later on today? Sure. That sounds like a great idea. We may as well get started."

For the next two weeks, I traveled to Kenosha daily, helping build Rich's customer base while he continued to work as a writer/producer for the corporation. When he got home, we worked well together, although I thought he was a bit stuffy at times.

All went well, until a situation developed which threatened to end our working relationship. I had teased him about his excitement and dedication toward building his own business, saying it was as fanatical as my search for my Perfect Spiritual Partner. The mood changed instantly. It was as though someone had dealt him a deadly blow. All the color left his face, and I was not sure just exactly what had happened or what I should do. When I inquired, he would only say that he had to think about whether we could continue to work together.

He left the room, and I was stunned. His words had seemed terminal. I had begun to believe he was the perfect partner I had long searched for, and now he was actually considering our parting company.

As I waited for him to return, I earnestly prayed that whatever was highest and best for both of us would occur. I surrendered to the idea that, even if he was my perfect spiritual partner, I would release him if he did not want to continue our relationship. After an hour, I knocked on his door. He would not tell me what had occurred, only that he felt it was possible for us to continue working together, despite the fact that we seemed to be headed in opposite directions. I was befuddled, but relieved.

We agreed to do some work in Milwaukee that weekend. I offered to let him sleep on my couch rather than travel back and forth each evening, and he accepted.

On Saturday evening, we decided to take a break to make popcorn and watch TV. As we sat on my couch, talking about the events of the day, Rich said, "Once in a while, I have wanted to put my arm around you and give you a hug."

I was taken aback by the idea and asked him why he felt that way. "Because I think you are great. And I just feel like hugging you."

I did not know what to say. Part of me already knew he was my perfect spiritual partner, but there was still a part of me seeing him as too tall, too thin, wrong color hair, and so on.

Then the biggest miracle of my life, to date, happened. He asked, "Well, can I give you a hug?"

"I guess so," was my weak reply.

For the next five hours, we sat silently embracing one another in the sweetest hug the world has ever known. We were enwrapped in the most beautiful, blissful feeling I have ever experienced. It was as if every part of our beings: bodies, minds and souls resounded in celebration of finding one another. Wave after wave of joy ran through our bodies, out into the ethers, and back to us. We were surrounded by joy; joy was in us, coursing through us, and acting as us. It was as if we *were* joy, and the whole atmosphere lifted a voice to echo that joy to the world. And I knew what true ecstasy is.

Not once, during those five hours, did the feeling of joy leave us. And not once did any sexual energy enter into the embrace. It was pure. It was holy. And it was the most real thing I had ever experienced.

Later, when I went to my bedroom to sleep, I remembered a dream I had three years earlier. I was sitting in the passenger seat of a small car. A man was driving, but I could not see his face or his body. All I could see was his right arm and hand, which was holding my left hand. In my dream I had felt so much joy and love in that simple act of holding hands. Now I understood the significance of the dream, and how it had foretold this future event: that I would recognize the one who was truly my ideal mate by the love and joy we would experience in our first embrace.

Now everything made sense. Here he was, my opposite and my twin. Yes, we had differences, but they were mostly superficial or inconsequential. The things that really counted, the things that meant the world to us, were where we agreed. Suddenly, I remembered hearing the words "three years" in my mind, as I drove for the first time from Michigan to Milwaukee, contemplating life with my perfect partner. It had been three years to the day, since I had heard those words.

I soon found out that even perfect spiritual partners have enough differences to make life enjoyable, interesting and challenging. One day Rich kept delaying our plans, and I could not understand why he had to meditate so long. When he finally came out of his room, he said, "I have been arguing with Divine Mother (as we sometimes refer to God) for two hours and forty-five minutes. Will you marry me?"

Not even a moment was required to think that one through, "I would be happy to marry you, Richard," was my immediate response. Then I asked, "What were you arguing with the Divine about?"

"I could not see why I had to ask you right now. We hardly even know one another."

A few days later, at the end of my meditation it came to me that we were supposed to buy an engagement ring that day. Richard had taken the day off from work so we could relax together. He said, "Let's go to Brookfield Square and window shop."

From his comment, I was sure he had gotten the same idea, but at the shopping center he ignored the jewelry stores unless I dragged him in. I was getting frustrated, and finally asked him, "Why did you want to come here in the first place?"

After several minutes of confrontation, I was growing even more frustrated, and wanted to leave. At this point, he admitted, "I am supposed to buy you an engagement ring, but I am resisting the idea."

He was purposely not following his inner guidance because of pressure from me to do so. I laughed out loud. That is why he had been acting so weird.

We hugged and strolled, arm in arm, beginning to shop in earnest. Nothing appealed to me. I suggested we go to Mayfair Mall. I took him directly to Fox Jewelry, and surveyed the display case to the far left. There it was: the same ring I had found two years earlier. It was still the most beautiful ring I had ever seen: solitary marquise diamond with filigree butterflies and hearts on both sides. I asked the saleswoman if I could try it on. As before, I inquired what the price would be with an amethyst instead of a diamond, since I had always wanted an amethyst ring. Richard saw where the questions were leading and said, "No. I am buying you a diamond engagement ring. Nothing less."

Although we both felt it was important to date for at least a year before marrying, my intuition kept saying, "October 15th." I did not understand why we had to marry after only knowing each other three months, but I had learned that the inner guidance is always right.

On September 15th we were on our way to Pennsylvania to meet my family. During the trip, I asked Richard why he had acted as if he had been shot with a bullet when I had mentioned my search for my perfect spiritual partner. He replied, "Because I could not figure out how you could be searching for your perfect partner, when it was me. And I could not understand why you didn't know it was me."

I asked him when he first knew we were ideal mates. "The first time we talked on the phone. As we hung up, the inner voice said, 'Karen Bowen, Karen Bowen,'" and I said, "Oh, no. I am not getting married again."

It is hard for me to admit that he knew it before I did.

We would have preferred to be married by Yogacharya at Song of the Morning in Michigan, but when we returned from our trip to Pennsylvania, we found a message on Rich's answering machine. Yogacharya Oliver had passed on September 16th, two weeks after his 96th birthday. We both sank to the couch in disbelief, sadness, and sorrow. A dear friend who loved us both, unconditionally, had left. We had attended his birthday party on September 1st. He had looked great, "like a teenager," Rich said. Neither of us had had any idea he would be leaving. At the end of September, we traveled to Detroit for a memorial service in his honor.

On October 15th, after knowing each other three months and having only one date, Richard and I were married by a Unity minister in Kenosha. We were required by law to have two witnesses, so we invited Rich's mother and one of his best friends. As we vowed always to be kind to one another and to treat one another with respect, we exchanged roses. I realized why a year-long engagement was not necessary, we already knew we were perfect for one another. We did not have to get to know each other to make sure it was the right decision. Later, we prepared a meal for our guests, as our first act of service as newlyweds. The next stage in our adventure had begun, we were eager, happy and excited to walk the path together.

Higher Love

Marriage to my perfect partner has been like no other experience I have ever had. Our life is different than yours will be. But let me tell you how we are.

Being twin souls means we are a pair. You can compare us to a pair of gloves. It is obvious which gloves match, but there are always differences between the right- and left-hand parts of the set. One may be more worn than the other, one may have a stitch loose in the thumb, one may have been soiled by a spill in the garden, one may have thorns in its side from the rose bush it helped to trim. Nonetheless, they are a pair. We are like that. It is obvious to us and to most people we meet that we are ideally mated.

I have always wanted a brave, noble and courageous man as my partner. When I met Rich, he did not look the part. But my experience has shown me that he is the most courageous man I have ever met, not only because he stands up for what he believes in, in the world, but also because he is willing to fight all the inner battles. Courage in facing outer circumstances is honorable. But I have watched my dearly beloved face inner demons that superman would run from.

Our life together is so sweet, it is sometimes difficult to find words to describe it. I know that we like and love each other much more now, than we did at first. We relish being with one another, whether we are working or playing.

So, what can I say about our relationship in a nutshell? It is the match made for us in heaven. It is the love beyond our wildest dreams. It is joy to know that we are home at last, safe in one another's arms. And all is well.

The truth is, there are not enough words in the world to describe the experience of being with your perfect partner. It is like trying to explain what an orange tastes like to someone who has never eaten one. You cannot. The person has to experience it himself. In the same way, all the descriptions in all the books in all the world can never truly relate something you have never experienced. Our story is true. If it can happen to us, it can certainly happen to you. The reason we are mates is because we are both courageous individuals, who refused to accept anything less than the perfect partner. The world needs individuals willing to make the effort, to add to the joy of the planet instead of the sadness. We pray, with all our hearts, you will join us.

To forgive and forget is a sign
of great strength and wisdom.
For, what you refuse to give another,
you cannot have for yourself.

Epilogue

It has been over two decades since we first published this book. The twists and turns our lives have taken since then amaze us both. We have been through trials we could not have envisioned, we have endured immense sadness, separation and reunion. We have learned new methods of healing the physical, emotional and mental bodies, as well as, powerful methods for changing limiting beliefs almost instantly.

Our journey together has taken on new meaning as we assist others in their process of discovery. I have developed workshops where I share much of what we have learned. And I am currently putting this information into another book.

If this book has been helpful please check out our current events and publications at:

www.karenabowen.com

About the Author

Karen A. Bowen's work includes assisting individuals with a variety of needs and backgrounds. Parents, children, couples, entrepreneurs, as well as, PhD's, and professionals all benefit from her ability to identify the limiting beliefs and obstacles preventing their success. Using the modalities of Energy Psychology, Radical Forgiveness and Esoteric Healing, Karen helps each individual remove the blocks, gain new insight, and reclaim their power to create the life they love.

Many know Karen as a wise and trusted mentor and friend.

She says, "I am present to remind each person of their power of creation and to assist them in removing whatever obstacles block their path to fulfilling their heart's desire."

Karen is also the originator of the Authentic Triangle™. She teaches numerous workshops, is a published author, and nationally known public speaker, whose special skill is to teach how life works and how to make spiritual laws practical in our everyday lives.

She lives in the Midwest with her pets and her husband Richard A. Bowen who is also an author.

For Information or an appointment, visit
www.karenabowen.com

www.ingramcontent.com/pod-product-compliance
Lightning Source LLC
Chambersburg PA
CBHW060239050426
42448CB00009B/1514